Native Americans of the Southeast

Christina M. Girod

Lucent Books, Inc.
P.O. Box 289011, San Diego, California

Titles in the Indigenous Peoples of North America Series Include:

The Apache
The Cherokee
The Cheyenne
The Comanche
The Iroquois
Native Americans of the Great Lakes
Native Americans of the Northeast
Native Americans of the Northwest Coast
Native Americans of the Plains
Native Americans of the Southeast
Native Americans of the Southwest
The Navajo
The Pawnee
The Sioux

Library of Congress Cataloging-in-Publication Data

Girod, Christina M.
  Native Americans of the Southeast / by Christina M. Girod.
    p. cm.—(Indigenous peoples of North America)
Includes bibliographical references and index.
Summary: Discusses the history, daily lives, culture, religion, and conflicts
of the Indians that lived in the southeastern region of the United States.
  ISBN 1-56006-610-5 (hardcover)
  1. Indians of North America—Southern States—Juvenile literature.
[1. Indians of North America—Southern States.] I. Title. II. Series.
  E78.S65 G57 2001
  975.004'97—dc21
                                                                    00-008654

Copyright 2001 by Lucent Books, Inc.
P.O. Box 289011, San Diego, California 92198-9011

Printed in the U.S.A.

Contents

Foreword

North America's native peoples are often relegated to history—viewed primarily as remnants of another era—or cast in the stereotypical images long found in popular entertainment and even literature. Efforts to characterize Native Americans typically result in idealized portrayals of spiritualists communing with nature or bigoted descriptions of savages incapable of living in civilized society. Lost in these unfortunate images is the rich variety of customs, beliefs, and values that comprised—and still comprise—many of North America's native populations.

The *Indigenous Peoples of North America* series strives to present a complex, realistic picture of the many and varied Native American cultures. Each book in the series offers historical perspectives as well as a view of contemporary life of individual tribes and tribes that share a common region. The series examines traditional family life, spirituality, interaction with other native and non-native peoples, warfare, and the ways the environment shaped the lives and cultures of North America's indigenous populations. Each book ends with a discussion of life today for the Native Americans of a given region or tribe.

In any discussion of the Native American experience, there are bound to be sim-

ilarities. All tribes share a past filled with unceasing white expansion and resistance that led to more than four hundred years of conflict. One U.S. administration after another pursued this goal and fought Indians who attempted to defend their homelands and ways of life. Although no war was ever formally declared, the U.S. policy of conquest precluded any chance of white and Native American peoples living together peacefully. Between 1780 and 1890, Americans killed hundreds of thousands of Indians and wiped out whole tribes.

The Indians lost the fight for their land and ways of life, though not for lack of bravery, skill, or a sense of purpose. They simply could not contend with the overwhelming numbers of whites arriving from Europe or the superior weapons they brought with them. Lack of unity also contributed to the defeat of the Native Americans. For most, tribal identity was more important than racial identity. This loyalty left the Indians at a distinct disadvantage. Whites had a strong racial identity and they fought alongside each other even when there was disagreement because they shared a racial destiny.

Although all Native Americans share this tragic history they have many distinct differences. For example, some tribes and individuals sought to cooperate almost immediately with the U.S. government while others steadfastly resisted the white presence. Life before the arrival of white settlers also varied. The nomads of the Plains developed altogether different lifestyles and customs from the fishermen of the Northwest coast.

Contemporary life is no different in this regard. Many Native Americans—forced onto reservations by the American government—struggle with poverty, poor health, and inferior schooling. But others have regained a sense of pride in themselves and their heritage, enabling them to search out new routes to self-sufficiency and prosperity.

The *Indigenous Peoples of North America* series attempts to capture the differences as well as similarities that make up the experiences of North America's native populations—both past and present. Fully documented primary and secondary source quotations enliven the text. Sidebars highlight events, personalities, and traditions. Bibliographies provide readers with ideas for further research. In all, each book in this dynamic series provides students with a wealth of information as well as launching points for further research.

Evolution of a People

The southeast region of North America comprises about four hundred thousand square miles of the United States. It stretches from the Mississippi River in the west to the Atlantic Ocean in the east, and from the Appalachian Mountains in the north to the Gulf of Mexico in the south. It includes the modern-day states of Florida, Georgia, South Carolina, Alabama, Mississippi, Louisiana, and parts of Tennessee and North Carolina.

The countryside is dotted by large industrial cities such as Birmingham, Mobile, Atlanta, and Charleston, as well as tourist centers like New Orleans, Orlando, and Tampa. Today chemicals, electronics, and textiles are mass-produced in the cities, and agricultural production of livestock, soybeans, tobacco, and peanuts reigns in the rural areas.

Most of the farms and towns in the Southeast are occupied by people of European, African, or Latino descent. But in the nearby hills of Appalachia, along the meandering rivers, and deep within the Florida wetlands, there still live groups of the region's original inhabitants. These are descendants of the indigenous peoples, or Native American tribes, of the Choctaw, Chickasaw, Cherokee, Calusa, Timucua, Catawba, Natchez, Creek, and Seminole, as well as many other smaller tribes.

The majority of these Native Americans live on reservations in Oklahoma, where their ancestors were forcibly removed in the 1830s. Others live on small reservations or private lands on or near their original homelands. Many have become part of mainstream America, living and working in cities and towns scattered all across the United States.

Native Americans had lived and prospered in the region for at least ten thousand years by the time the first Europeans encountered them in the early sixteenth century. In that time great civilizations like the ancient mound-builder culture had developed highly complex systems of agriculture, commerce, religion, and government. These people lived in highly organized societies where the daily responsibilities of hunting, farming, war, spiritual guidance, and creative expression were interlinked with a profound respect for the earth. David Ipinia, a Yurok artist, reflects this philosophy in a comment:

> Being an Indian is mainly in your heart. It's a way of walking with the earth instead of upon it. A lot of the history books talk about us Indians in the past tense, but we don't plan on going anywhere. We have lost so much, but the thing that holds us together is that we all belong to and are protectors of the earth; that's the reason for us being here. Mother Earth is not a resource, she is an heirloom.[1]

The Arrival of the Europeans

The first Europeans to contact the indigenous people of the Southeast were Spanish explorers and missionaries, closely followed by French traders and more missionaries. About one hundred years later, English traders and colonists entered the region. The earliest explorers plundered, killed, and enslaved hundreds of Native Americans in their quest for gold and treasure. The missionaries converted whole tribes to Christianity, which had the effect of extinguishing many cultural attributes. In addition, the Europeans introduced diseases such as smallpox, cholera, and malaria, to which Native Americans had no immunity, resulting in thousands of deaths. As Native Americans acquired more and more trade goods, they began to be dependent on the Europeans and their wares, and lost many of their cultural traditions as well as their self-sufficiency.

A member of the Seminole tribe living in Florida.

Language on the Map

The languages of the people of the Southeast were rich and varied. Much of their vocabulary has been preserved in the names of cities, towns, lakes, rivers, and states. Cities like Biloxi, Tuskegee, Chickamauga, Tallahassee, Tampa, and Miami, which means "that place," are named for particular tribes or words derived from their languages. Tuscaloosa, Alabama, is named for a Choctaw chief who lived in the region in the 1500s.

"Mississippi" and "Tennessee" both come from Native American words, while Alabama takes its name from the Alabamu people who inhabited the central portion of the state. Apalachee Bay, whose name means "people of the other side," owes its name to the people who once lived on its shores. Lake Okeechobee in Florida got its name from a Muskogee word meaning "big water," as did the Chattahoochee River, which means "marked stones."

Because pre-Columbian Native Americans did not have a written language, our knowledge about their early life is limited to firsthand accounts recorded by Europeans, who understood little of their cultures and judged them in the context of European standards. Even in the twentieth century the image of the Native American was tainted by European biases about what constitutes "civilized" behavior. The people were portrayed in American books and films as bloodthirsty savages. In addition, much of what was recorded about the tribes was done only after they had begun an intense effort to adopt European ways of life, in a vain effort to appease land-hungry white settlers who were ready to use the "civilization" issue as an excuse for taking over tribal lands.

Although most people of the Southeast had been farmers for centuries, Europeans chose to ignore the Native Americans' agricultural expertise and justified their continual seizure of tribal territories by asserting that the land was not being put to its best use. Wave after wave of settlers pushed the native peoples farther inland, and they found themselves forced to give up more and more land through treaties. Many of these agreements were unfair, even illegal, and those that included provisions for just treatment of the tribes were seldom honored. Eventually most Native Americans of the Southeast were forced to leave their ancestral lands under humiliating and tragic circumstances.

Since the mid–nineteenth century, Native Americans have struggled to survive on the reservations. Plagued by poor health, alcoholism, and poverty, their populations plummeted. High unemployment rates and a lack of education contributed to the sense of hopelessness that many people suffered. A growing dependence on welfare and government subsidies deprived them of a sense of pride and their cultural identity.

Regaining a Sense of Identity

Despite the recent centuries of hardship that Native Americans of the Southeast have endured, they are today reclaiming their heritage and dignity. Elders are making an effort to increase awareness of cultural traditions among the younger generation, including a revival of appreciation for and practice of native arts,

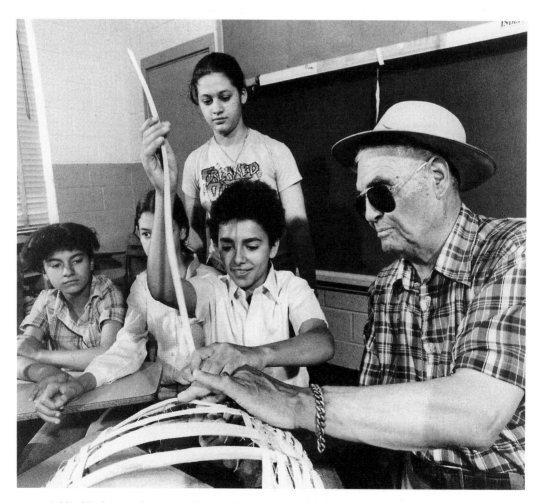

A blind Indian craftsman teaches students to weave baskets as part of an Indian education program in the public schools of Robeson County, North Carolina.

languages, festivals, and spiritual beliefs.

A recent movement called Pan-Indianism has successfully united Native Americans from all over North America under a common identity as First Americans. They are strengthening their resolve to be respected as an ethnic group in their own right. Rachel Snow, an Assiniboine, explains why unity among Native Americans is so important: "I come to a powwow to be an Indian, to get a sense of myself. This is part of Indian spiri-tuality, to help each other and to celebrate with each other. When I come to powwows, I gain strength to carry on with my life."[2]

Many tribes are participating more in government in an effort to support the rights of Native Americans, to enforce past agreements, and to regain ancestral homelands. They are trying to ensure the survival not just of their people, but also of their heritage. Indeed, the Native Americans of the Southeast are looking into the future with hope in their hearts.

Chapter 1

Native Peoples of the Southeast

The first people who settled in the southeastern region of what is today the United States arrived from the western part of North America around 8000 B.C. They found a country with a wonderfully temperate climate, brimming with lush plant growth and abundant wildlife.

There were small mammals such as rabbit, opossum, otter, and raccoon, as well as herds of larger species like deer, bear, and bison. Both fresh- and saltwater fish thrived in the Atlantic Ocean, the rivers, and the lakes, while migratory birds and waterfowl regularly visited the forests and wetlands.

At first the people who inhabited the southeastern region lived a nomadic life as hunters and gatherers. About 300 B.C. they began to farm and adopted a more sedentary lifestyle, developing many diverse languages, customs, and beliefs. They were farmers, hunters, fishermen, artisans, and warriors, with recognized political and spiritual leaders. Most fell into loosely associated confederations, or groups, of tribes. The people of the Southeast had a rich and varied culture, as described by Creek historians in "Muskoke Customs and Traditions:"

> Daily life was full of magic and mystery, but the importance of ritual was tempered by an equally strong belief in reason and justice. Harmony and balance have always been two very important concepts. . . . They are exemplified even within the earliest social structures as the . . . people combined work and play, religion and politics, and respect for nature as both a teacher and a supplier of needs.[3]

In the Appalachian highlands lived the Cherokee and the Catawba. On the coastal plains to the south lived Creek peoples like the Yamasee, Hitchiti, Apalachee, and the Alabamu. In the west lived the Chickasaw and the Choctaw, who according to which were formerly Creek territory. For centuries the Cherokee fought the Creek to the south, the Choctaw to the west, and the Shawnee in the north to protect their boundaries.

Cherokee territory stretched from the Ohio River in the north to the headwaters of the Savannah River in the south. The nearly forty-three thousand square miles covered parts of the states of Kentucky, Tennessee, North and South Carolina, Virginia, Alabama, and Georgia. The outlying lands were considered hunting grounds, while the rugged interior Great Smoky Mountains were lived upon and farmed.

With about eighteen thousand members, the Cherokee were one of the most numerous tribes in the Southeast, surpassed only by the Choctaw. There was no official seat of government. According to Samuel Carter III in his book *Cherokee Sunset*, "Their government . . . was merely a loose confederation of towns, each with its elected chief and local Council. There was no central government, no principal chief. The Cherokees' love of liberty and independence would have rejected any such despotism."[4]

Cherokee law was upheld by personal or family discipline. If this failed, a disputed issue would be resolved by the Council. Character was the most important factor in Cherokee law. The eighteenth-century botanist William Bartram described the Cherokee:

Two Cherokee boys converse in North Carolina, a state that was once partially covered by Cherokee Territory.

legend were once one tribe. Along the Mississippi were the Natchez, and nearby on the Alabama River were the Biloxi. The Timucua inhabited the coastal lowlands of northern Florida, while to the south the Calusa made their homes in the Everglades and the Florida Keys.

Tribes of the Appalachian Highlands

The Cherokee and the Catawba were the two major tribes that inhabited the Appalachian highlands. The Cherokee spoke an Iroquoian language and called themselves *Tsa-la-gi*, which means "principal people." Long ago driven out of the north—possibly the Great Lakes region—by their "grandfathers" the Delaware, they settled in the Blue Ridge Mountains,

The Great Smokies

The Great Smoky Mountains form the western portion of the Appalachian Mountains in the eastern United States. They stretch from western North Carolina to eastern Tennessee and overlap with the Blue Ridge Mountains to the east.

Some of the highest Appalachian peaks are in the Great Smokies, including the 6,643-foot-high Clingmans Dome, the highest point in Tennessee. There are five other peaks that reach over 6,000 feet high in the Great Smokies.

Most of the region is forested and is home to rhododendron, mountain laurel, and many wildflowers. Wildlife such as deer, elk, and bear also populated the Great Smokies. The region was home to the Cherokee tribe, who lived and farmed in the mountains and hunted in the surrounding lowlands.

In the mid-1800s two geologists, Senator Thomas L. Clingman and Arnold Guyot, explored the region. The Great Smokies were subsequently named for their characteristic haze.

Today the Great Smokies are a popular tourist area. The most rugged portion lies in the Great Smoky Mountains National Park, while hikers can traverse the Appalachian Trail, and motorists may enjoy the mountain scenery along the Blue Ridge Parkway.

The picturesque Great Smoky Mountains were once home to the Cherokee.

[I]n their disposition and manner [they] are grave and steady; dignified and circumspect in their deportment; rather slow and reserved in conversation; yet frank, cheerful and humane; tenacious of their liberties and natural rights of men; secret, deliberate and determined in their councils; honest, just and liberal and are ready always to sacrifice every pleasure and gratification, even their blood, and life itself, to defend their territory and maintain their rights.[5]

These rights extended to women as well, who often held positions of high status in the Council. Such women were called *Ghighau* or "beloved woman," and their advice was sought regularly on civil and war policy.

The Catawba lived to the east of the Blue Ridge Mountains in North and South Carolina in the foothills. They were Siouan-speaking and less numerous, with five thousand members. The Catawba defended their home from the Delaware in the north and the Shawnee who raided them from the northwest. A town chief and his council led Catawba villages. A principal town united all the Catawba under a loose central administration.

Tribes of the Coastal Plains

The largest tribe of the southeastern coastal plains was the Creek, a loose confederacy organized much like the Cherokee. The major group of the Creek Confederacy was the Muskogee, who migrated to Alabama and Georgia from the west around A.D. 800 and conquered or formed alliances with the tribes already present. They spoke Muskogee, which is a principal Native American tongue.

The Creek tribe also included other Muskogean-speaking groups. The Yamasee lived in north Florida, south Georgia, and southern South Carolina. The Hitchiti occupied seven large towns in north Florida and south Georgia. The Apalachee originally lived on the lower Chattahoochee River in north Florida near present-day Tallahassee. They joined the confederacy in the 1700s after being nearly destroyed by the Creek and the English. The Alabamu were a small group that lived in central Alabama. The non-Muskogean-speaking Yuchi were a small group that originally lived in eastern Tennessee and north Georgia.

The Choctaw were a Muskogean-speaking people who inhabited eastern Mississippi, Louisiana, and western Alabama. In the seventeenth century the tribe had over twenty thousand members, living in forty-five towns, making it the largest Native American tribe in the Southeast. They were the only group in the region to harvest a crop surplus so great that they traded the excess to neighboring tribes.

The Choctaw were divided into three political districts, each governed by an elected *mingo,* or principal chief, and a district council. A *mingo* earned his status through being a person of sound character, admired by all. The *mingo* had the power to call the Council at any time to

The Government of the Creek Confederacy

The Creek Confederacy was made up of about fifty self-governing towns with a total population of fifteen thousand to twenty thousand members. The confederacy created a powerful force against enemies such as the Chickasaw and the Cherokee. Donald Worcester, in his book *Forked Tongues and Broken Treaties*, describes the workings of the confederacy:

"Creek history is a splendid example of democracy in action. Despite the different elements that made up the Confederacy, the Creeks thought of themselves as one people united against enemy tribes located nearby. . . . In the early years, however, the Confederacy was loosely governed by leaders in the historic towns of Coweta, Cussita, Tuckabatchee, and Coosa. The people were held together by the ties of language, intermarriage between clans, frequent regional council meetings, and an annual national Council."

Although there was no central capital, there were four principal towns. The unofficial capital was the town of the chief, or *micco*, who presided over the national council, whose membership changed every year.

Each Creek town was governed by a *micco* who was known by his town name rather than his personal name. The *micco* presided over the town council and was assisted by a *micco apotka*, or twin chief. Both the *micco* and the Council were responsible for making the town laws. Another group of officials known as *henchas* was responsible for public works, fieldwork, and ceremonies.

A Creek town also had several war officials who did not participate in the civil administration. The war leader was called the *tastanage*, and below him were three levels of other officials who earned their titles by performing great deeds in battle.

When a Creek town reached five hundred people it would split, and half of the residents would move to a nearby site. Here, a new ceremonial center would be built with new homes around it, and new council members and officials would be chosen. A "mother-daughter" relationship would flourish between the old and the new, strengthening the ties of the confederacy.

All Creek towns were divided into red, or war, towns and white, or peace, towns. The designation as red or white was traditional and not related to the social temperament of a town. Neither was it permanent, as a town could change its affiliation for various reasons. Usually *miccos* were chosen from white towns and war officials were chosen from red towns.

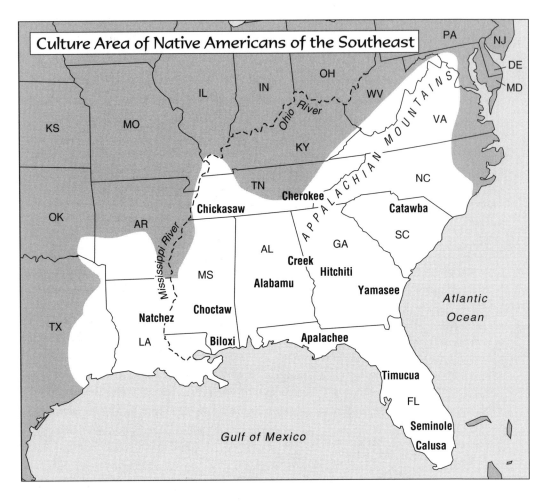

Culture Area of Native Americans of the Southeast

discuss public policy or to rule on important issues. An assistant *mingo* was responsible for public works, ceremonies, and festivals. At the town level, captains and subcaptains administered the law. Each town also had a war chief and two assistants. A national council was called in matters of tribal crisis, presided over by a *mingo*.

The Chickasaw were also Muskogean-speaking, and their language was almost identical to Choctaw. They occupied the region between the Mississippi River on the west side and the Tennessee and Mobile Rivers on the east side. Their territory covered northern Mississippi, western Tennessee, and parts of Alabama and Kentucky.

Less numerous than the Choctaw, the Chickasaw were known for being fierce warriors, the "unconquered and the unconquerable." They were constantly at war with their neighbors the Creek, the Cherokee to the east, the Shawnee to the north, and the

Osage from the plains to the west. The Chickasaw were also renowned traders and controlled the commerce on the Mississippi River. Once their language had been the universal language of trade in the Southeast.

The Natchez, non-Muskogean speakers who lived in the lower Mississippi River region near present-day Natchez, Mississippi, were a small tribe, possibly the last remnant of the Mississippian mound-builder culture. Unlike the other southeastern peoples, the Natchez had a god-king, called the Great Sun, who exercised absolute authority over the tribe.

Many other smaller tribes lived on the southeastern coastal plains, but most disappeared soon after the arrival of Europeans in the 1500s. Unfortunately, very little was written about these peoples. One such tribe was the Biloxi, a small Siouan-speaking group who lived in southeastern Mississippi. Destroyed by disease, slavery, and warfare, the few who survived were scattered among other tribes, and soon lost all connection to their former culture and language.

The Florida Tribes

The Timucua, who had a population of thirteen thousand in 1650, inhabited northern Florida and part of southeastern Georgia. They spoke a language unrelated to any other known language and may have had as many as nine dialects. Their name is derived from *thimogona*, a Timucua word meaning "my enemy."

The Timucua were organized into thirty to forty politically allied chiefdoms, each made up of several villages.

Each village was directed by a *holata,* or chief, an *inija,* or assistant chief, and several council members. All chiefs were chosen from the White Deer clan and the title was passed from uncle to sister's son. It was also possible for women to become chiefs, but how the title was passed in such a case is unclear. Respected elders and villagers of high status were called principal men and principal women. They served as advisers to the chief and the council. Each chief was supported by a *paracusi,* or war chief, and his advisers.

Chiefdoms were formed when a village grew too large to sustain its population. Some residents would then branch out to start a new village. The original village was considered to be a principal town. All the village *holatas* and councils selected a high chief from a principal town to lead the chiefdom. Loose alliances were formed between chiefdoms through intermarriage and to defeat common enemies.

Like the Timucua, the Calusa spoke a language whose origin is unknown. This tribe of ten thousand members lived in southern Florida below present-day Tampa, including the Florida Keys. The Calusa had almost disappeared by 1700, before historians had recorded enough of their language to study it. There may have been as many as twenty-four different languages spoken, possibly of Muskogean origin.

Again like the Timucua, the Calusa lived in villages organized into chiefdoms.

The Florida Everglades

The Everglades are located in southern Florida, from Lake Okeechobee in the north to the Gulf of Mexico. The Everglades encompass a limestone basin that is covered by mostly saw grass, which grows ten to fifteen feet high, its narrow leaves edged with sharp, toothlike points. Some areas are open water, others are marshy, and there are also many hammocks, which are low islands. The hammocks are home to palms, pines, live oaks, cypresses, saw palmettos, and other trees and shrubs. Some of the marshy areas once grew papaw and morning glories.

An abundance of wildlife makes its home in the Everglades. Wading birds such as herons, egrets, and ibis are found in the region. Alligators, turtles, and various snakes also live in the wetlands. On the hammocks there were once large populations of deer, wildcats, pumas, bears, and several smaller animals.

The climate of the Everglades is tropical or subtropical, depending largely on the southeast trade winds. Rainfall is usually more than fifty-five inches per year. The average daily temperature ranges from a low of sixty-three degrees in January to a high of eighty-two degrees in July.

The Calusa tribe lived in the Everglades before the arrival of Europeans. They called it *Pa-May-Okee* or "Grassy Water." The Calusa lived on the hammocks and hunted and fished in the swamps and marshes. Later the Seminole made the area home.

In the twentieth century drainage projects destroyed many species' habitats. Canals from Lake Okeechobee have transformed one-fifth of the region to agricultural land. In 1947 the Everglades National Park was established to protect the ecosystem and land of the south central region. Today environmentalists including Native Americans are attempting to preserve the remainder of the Everglades through legislation.

The Everglades, once home to the Calusa and the Seminole, teems with wildlife.

There were nearly thirty chiefdoms, of which five were principal. A principal chief, or *calos,* governed each chiefdom. The Calusa were the only southeastern people who did not farm. The rich fish and plant life of the region allowed them to obtain all the nutrients they needed to survive without having to cultivate corn or other staple crops.

The political systems of the Native American tribes of the Southeast allowed them to evolve complex social relationships that united them both within a community and within a family unit.

Chapter 2

Villages and Clans of the Southeast Peoples

The extremely long, warm season allowed the people of the Southeast to grow two crops of corn each year. The temperate climate also meant that the hunting seasons were prolonged, and various edible plants could be gathered almost year-round. The ease with which the earth's abundance was available to the tribes contributed to the development of highly organized towns and villages.

Villages of the Southeastern Tribes

By the sixteenth century the southeastern region was bustling with hundreds of agrarian towns that served both the political and spiritual needs of the people that lived there. Despite some political and geographical differences, the tribes of the area lived and worked in towns that were organized in very similar ways.

Towns were typically located near or on a body of water, such as on the seacoast, near a delta, or along a lake or river. Having water nearby made watering crops and

traveling for hunting or trade expeditions easier. The number of residences per town varied greatly. Creek towns had anywhere from twenty-five to one hundred houses. The larger towns always had a ceremonial plaza at their center. Many smaller towns did not have a ceremonial center but were politically allied with a larger town, where people traveled for important ceremonies or political events.

The square central plaza contained a round structure made of poles and mud-daubed walls as well as an open summer house made of poles. Both structures were used for council meetings. In the middle of the plaza the sacred fire was located. In "Muskoke Customs and Traditions," Creek historians report:

> Each [town] possessed a "sacred fire" which had been given to them in the beginning, and was kept and rekindled periodically. This fire was considered to be a physical link connecting humankind and the Great

Spirit. The fire supplied heat and light for both the household and the community ceremonies. . . . The sun and the sacred fire within the ceremonial ring . . . are the same. . . . The fire, like an ancestor or tribal elder, must be treated with respect.[6]

Nearby was the sweat lodge where people went for purification and healing. A large adjoining yard was used for playing popular games such as stickball. Throughout the year, the plaza was filled with the sounds of people gathering for dances, ceremonies, and day-to-day socializing.

Surrounding the plaza were the homes and family compounds of the *micco*, the spiritual and military officials, and other persons of status. The outlying buildings were the houses and storage bins of the general public. The homes were connected to each other and to the central plaza by a network of trails.

Natchez towns were similar, but the ceremonial center was built upon a square, flat-topped mound rather than in a plaza. The Great Sun's home as well as other houses were also built on top of mounds in precise rows around the ceremonial mound. Scattered family farms and larger crops surrounded the mounds.

The Florida tribes lived in much smaller villages of about twenty to thirty homes each. Houses were surrounded by family

An illustration depicts the thatched-roofed, open-sided houses built by the Seminole in the late nineteenth century.

corncribs and storage bins, work areas, and drying racks for meat. As elsewhere in the Southeast, the houses surrounded a central plaza where ceremonial and political events took place.

Clans of the Creek Confederacy

Although the Native American tribes of the Southeast made their homes in towns and villages, the residents themselves were divided into clans, or groups of people who claimed a common ancestry. They determined ancestry matrilineally—that is, by tracing from mother to grandmother, and so on, back through the generations.

Clan loyalty was strong, superseding loyalty to a town. Since, however, not all members of a clan lived in the same town or village, clan loyalties linked many communities together. Moreover, because marriage between members of the same clan was considered incest, punishable by death, many young people took spouses from other towns, a practice that established or strengthened blood alliances between communities.

Alliances of one clan with another were not unusual, creating yet another layer of allegiance. Some alliances were formed by marriage or in recognition of a traditional connection celebrated in common myths. In other cases, clans joined together to defeat a common enemy or to share a common exploit. For example, men from two or more different clans residing in the same town might organize a single large hunting expedition where all members of

the group cooperated to achieve a common goal—that is, obtaining meat and hides to feed and clothe their families through the winter.

Perhaps not surprisingly, the tradition that placed clan loyalty above town loyalty sometimes caused towns to be torn apart. Blood feuds between members of different clans might pit one town against another or, worse, cause divisions within a single town. Increasing this potential for trouble was the revenge system, which was a basic norm of clan behavior in the southeastern tribes.

Revenge: A Powerful Clan Tradition

When a crime was committed, the victim's clan held the wrongdoer's entire clan responsible. The general rule was an eye for an eye and blood for blood; it did not matter whether the person on whom revenge was exacted was the actual perpetrator of the crime.

The revenge system, which strikes many modern observers as inherently unfair, was not in fact designed to promote fairness. "Rather than justice," as Cherokee writer Michael Rutledge explains, "the Cherokee system was ideal for keeping balance and harmony in the spiritual and social worlds." He continues by recounting a tribal myth that reveals these connections:

> One day, some Cherokee children were playing outside, when a rattlesnake crawled out of the grass. They screamed and their mother ran

Clans and Totems

The name of a clan also identified the clan's totem. The totem was not an object of worship, but actually a guardian spirit and protector of the clan. It was taboo for clan members to kill, eat, or even touch their totem. The totem played an important role in clan mythology, such as a Creek clan myth in which the alligator totem played a role. This version of the traditional story appears in *Indians of the Southeast*, by Jesse Burt and Robert B. Ferguson. The story explains

"how the alligator obtained his crooked nose in a ball game with an unidentified variety of bird. The bird, which in one myth is described as monstrously large with great flapping wings, had possession of the ball and sought, most unfairly, to eliminate alligator from the game by dropping the ball from his beak on alligator's head. Alligator, however, avoided the main impact of the dropped ball by alertly dodging so that the ball descended on his nose. Though alligator suffered intense pain, for his nose was broken, he courageously seized and gripped the ball."

A totem crafted by the Miccosukee of the Florida Everglades. The totem represents a spirit that protects the clan.

outside. Without thinking, she took a stick and killed it.

Her husband was hunting in the mountains. As he was returning home that night, he heard a strange wailing sound. . . . [H]e found himself in the midst of a gathering of rattlesnakes, whose mouths were open and crying.

"What is the matter," the man asked the snakes. The rattlesnakes responded, "Your wife killed our chief, the Yellow Rattlesnake today. We are preparing to send the Black Rattlesnake to take revenge."

The husband immediately accepted their claim and took responsibility for the crime. The rattlesnakes said, "If you speak the truth, you must be ready to make satisfaction." The price they demanded was the life of his wife in sacrifice for that of their chief. . . .

The rattlesnakes told the man that the Black Rattlesnake would follow him home and coil up outside his door. He was to ask his wife to bring him a fresh drink of water from the spring. . . .

When the man reached home, it was very dark. His wife had supper waiting for him.

"Please bring me some water," he asked her. She brought him a gourd from the jar, but he refused it.

"No," he said. "I would like some fresh water from the spring."

His wife took a bowl and stepped outside to get him some fresh water. The man immediately heard her cry. He went outside and found the Black Rattlesnake had bitten her and she was already dying. He stayed with her until she was dead.

The Black Rattlesnake then crawled out of the grass. "My tribe is now satisfied," he told the husband.[7]

Other Clan Traditions

The clan system was not focused entirely on keeping order by means of revenge. Welfare was an important consideration, and it was common for clan members to offer hospitality to fellow members who were less fortunate. The widowed, disabled, or elderly could go from town to town and receive lodging and food from members of their own clan. People could also expect to receive continuing clan support within the town of their residence.

Some of the southeastern clans shared the practice of naming themselves after animals, birds, plants, and, occasionally, physical characteristics. For example, the Creek Confederacy consisted of nearly fifty clans, including Alligator, Cane, Fish, Salt, Medicine, and Arrow. Three of the principal Creek clans were Wind, Bear, and Eagle.

The Cherokee were divided into seven sacred clans. These were Bird, Wolf, Deer, Paint, Blue, Long Hair, and Wild Potato.

The Little Brother of War

The Little Brother of War was what the people of the Southeast called their most popular game, stickball, so named for its characteristic ferocity. Its major purpose was to settle disagreements between tribal towns.

Stickball was played using two wooden sticks bent into loops at one end and laced with rawhide strips to form a cup. The ball, about the size of a golf ball, was made of deer hide stuffed with deer hair. The game was played on a long field, with goals made from a broad post or two poles set apart at each end.

The number of players varied, but there had to be an even count between the two teams. The object of the game was to pass the ball to a goal. The first team to score twelve goals won. The rules varied between tribes, with some allowing the use of hands to throw the ball and some requiring it to be tossed with a stick. Stickball was incredibly rough, and could include pushing, shoving, pulling, butting, biting, choking, or gouging. When a player was knocked out, his opponent had to leave the game to keep the team numbers even.

In *Indians of the Southeast*, Jesse Burt and Robert B. Ferguson quote George Catlin, who visited and painted many Native American peoples in the early nineteenth century, about the lengthy preparations for stickball:

"The game had been arranged . . . three or four months before. . . . The two champions who led the two parties . . . sent runners, with the ball-sticks most fantastically ornamented with ribbons and red paint, to be touched by each one of the chosen players; who thereby agreed to be on the spot at the appointed time and ready for the play. The ground having been all prepared and preliminaries of the game all settled, and goods all 'staked,' night came."

The night before a game, the players fasted and observed other purification rituals. Spirits of powerful animals such as the panther were invoked so that the players might gain its strength. The flesh of rabbits or other weak animals was avoided, but the raccoon was consumed for its cunning. There was much dancing and singing. Catlin observed the dancing players "in their ball-play dress; rattling their ball-sticks together in the most violent manner, and all singing as loud as they could raise their voices. . . . This dance . . . was repeated at intervals of every half hour during the night, and exactly in the same manner; so that the players were certainly awake all the night." During this dance, the women would place bets on their household goods, men's weapons, and other items.

The game began at midmorning with a medicine man tossing the ball into the air between the team leaders. The players immediately threw themselves upon the ball. People in the audience ran along the perimeter of the field roaring at the players. When the game finally ended, the wagers were awarded to the victorious team.

The Timucua had clans called Panther, Bear, Fish, Earth, Buzzard, and Quail, in addition to the prestigious White Deer clan and others of lesser importance.

Other tribes were organized in a sort of class hierarchy, as exemplified by the family clans or *iksa*, of the Choctaw. The highest level was that of the *mingos* and war chiefs. Second in importance were the *Atacoulitoupa* or "beloved men" and "beloved women." Third were the *tasca* or warriors. Last in status were the supporting men who had never struck a blow in war, or who had killed women or children, but no other warriors.

The clans of the Natchez were also hierarchical. The nobility consisted of suns (relatives of their leader, the Great Sun), nobles, and honored ones. A noble had to marry a person of lower rank, but since class membership, like clan identity, was inherited from the mother, the status of the children was determined by whether the higher ranking spouse was the husband or wife. Thus, when a male sun married a commoner, the couple's child would be a noble, the rank immediately below sun; but the child of a female sun and a commoner would have sun status, like the mother. Classes were not permanent, however. A commoner could achieve noble status by performing honorable deeds.

Most Native Americans of the Southeast, regardless of clan affiliation or class status, observed similar conventions with respect to the roles of men and women and raised their children according to the same principles.

Traditional Roles of Men, Women, and Children

The Choctaw exemplified the roles of people in many of the southeastern tribes, designating women as the "keepers of life" and men as the "keepers of death." Indeed women prepared and cooked the food that sustained the people. They made clothing, storage containers for food, and other items. They gathered wild plants to eat, tended the crops, and brought in water. Most importantly, women gave birth to and raised children. By contrast, men cleared fields and felled trees. They created weapons and tools, and they directed civil law and spiritual events. Men built houses and constructed canoes. Most importantly, they served as warriors and hunters who protected and provided for the people.

Native American women of the Southeast were quite liberated compared to their European counterparts. Women owned the majority of property, including the house, fields, and crops. Men could lay claim only to their weapons, personal clothing, and a bowl used for meals.

Because children belonged to the mother's clan, the father did not play a large part in raising children. Rather, the mother's closest male relatives filled this role, usually her children's uncles.

Up to age three or four, Native American children of the Southeast spent most of their time running freely about the village, playing games, and listening to tribal legends retold by clan elders. After this time, boys and girls were separated and given tasks that were meant to prepare them for adult life.

Boys were instructed by the oldest maternal uncle in skills necessary for both hunting and war. Games and contests of archery, wrestling, running, ball play, and the throwing stick developed both strength and agility. Often boys would accompany uncles on hunting or fishing trips.

The oldest maternal aunt or the maternal grandmother taught the girls. They practiced the techniques for creating pottery and basketry, and helped their mothers prepare meals. Girls learned how to tan hides and make clothing. They also accompanied

A Seminole family cooks over a fire in the Everglades. Women traditionally tended crops and gathered plants in addition to preparing meals.

their female relatives in the fields and helped to tend the crops.

Despite these duties, children still enjoyed ample free time for playing with friends and for individual pursuits. Discipline was managed by words and by the example adults set for them. Very rarely was corporal punishment ever used. James Adair, an English trader who lived with the Southeast tribes for forty years, wrote about this type of discipline:

> The chief manly virtues were honor, and love of country, or the tribe, which were "prized above life." Feminine qualities were "a mild, amiable, soft disposition: exceedingly modest . . . and very seldom noisy, either in the single, or [married] state." This character molding in the young was accomplished mainly by sweet words. For instance, a boy who disgraced himself by cowardice would be praised by [his] uncle for his exemplary courage. . . . "I have known them to strike their delinquents with those sweetened darts (words), so good naturedly and skillfully, that they would sooner die by torture, than renew their shame by repeating the actions."[8]

A Cherokee woman shapes a clay pot.

Native Americans understood that high expectations in training children were the only guarantee that traditions would be passed on to successive generations, thus preserving the day-to-day life as their people had always known it.

Chapter 3

Daily Life Among the People of the Southeast

Native Americans of the Southeast were busy all year long performing the tasks that made survival possible. Summers were spent fishing, hunting waterfowl, and gathering berries. Crops were tended and houses repaired for the coming winter. The men were free to participate in war raids to avenge old wrongs.

In the fall, the crops were harvested and stored in bins for the winter, and large hunting expeditions were carried out. Those who were left in town busied themselves gathering nuts and fruits in the woods and along the riverbanks. Small groups of people came and went from the mountains and as far away as the Great Lakes in the north to trade wares.

During the early winter the hunters returned and the women were occupied drying meat and tanning hides. The men repaired and made new tools and weapons. During the long dark hours of the cold season the people gathered to hear traditional stories.

In the spring, fields were prepared and new crops planted, and the cycle of life began all over again.

Seasonal Hunting

Native Americans of the Southeast hunted throughout the year, but large game was sought during the late fall so that the people would have plenty of meat and warm hides to sustain them through the winter. During the warm season small game such as rabbit, raccoon, squirrel, quail, and prairie chicken were commonly hunted. The larger game consisted of the white-tailed deer, black bear, bison, alligator, and wild turkey.

White-tailed deer were by far the most abundant game animal. In the forests, herds of more than two hundred deer could be found. They were hunted by using decoys made of deerskin and antlers and by making special deer calls. Native Americans used all parts of the deer, leaving no waste. The skin and fur were

Crouching under their disguises, Florida Indians prepare to shoot their quarry. The decoy hunters wore deerskins and antlers and used deer calls to aid in the hunt.

used for clothing and bedding, while the meat, called venison, and insides were eaten.

Bears were also considered valuable. Bear fat was used as cooking oil or applied to the skin to keep out the winter cold. Bear hide made a warm, comfortable winter robe or blanket. A single bear could provide enough meat for a whole family during the winter.

Native Americans of the Southeast utilized many different kinds of weapons in hunting. Knives, blowguns, throwing sticks, clubs, traps, and snares were used to catch small game. Larger animals were hunted with the bow and arrow and with spears. Most weapons were fashioned from stone, shell, wood, feathers, and cane.

Blowguns, unique to the southeast region, were created from hollowed eight-to-ten-foot lengths of river cane. The darts were made from thin locust wood shafts with tufts of thistledown tied along the length of one end. The opposite end was sharpened into a fine point.

Although hunting was a necessity for survival, the lives of the animals were accorded great respect and their gifts were not taken for granted.

Hunting Taboos

Many taboos and rituals had to be observed in order to ensure the success of a hunt. These rituals protected the delicate balance between the earth's gifts and the needs of the people. The people were reminded of this balance through stories such as one that describes how animals and people had once lived together in peace. Over time, people invented weapons and hunted the animals, who grew upset about the killing. The animals decided that any person who killed an animal was required to ask its spirit for forgiveness. If a hunter failed to ask for the animal's pardon he would be afflicted with rheumatism. All hunters were taught forgiveness prayers that would appease a slain animal's spirit and allow its soul to be reborn. One such prayer, commonly chanted by Choctaw hunters, went as follows: "Deer, I am sorry to hurt you, but the people are hungry."[9]

When a young man returned from his first successful hunt for bear, deer, or wild turkey, he could not eat of its flesh. The occasion was instead celebrated as a ritual renewal of the bond between people and animals. Before embarking on a hunt, hunters fasted, prayed, and called to the spirit of the intended game with a ceremonial song. Following a purification ritual, the hunters danced and sang beautiful songs such as this Hitchiti (Creek) song, which called the spirit of the deer:

Somewhere the deer lies on the ground. I think; I walk about.

A Cherokee hunter uses a blowgun, a weapon unique to the Southeast tribes.

31

The Appearance of the Southeast Peoples

Deerskin was the most common material from which clothing was made. Bear, bison, and smaller animal hides were also popular. The skins were scraped and cleaned of hair, then rubbed with deer brains in a process called tanning. This created soft leather, which was cut into pieces and stitched together with plant fibers threaded on bone needles. Taylor and Sturtevant, in *The Native Americans: The Indigenous People of North America,* describe the different types of garments worn by southeastern people:

"Daily clothing . . . was a simple affair. Women wore knee-length skirts and men wore breechclouts, and both usually went without upper garments. They wore leggings which are long, wide pieces of single cloth wrapped around each leg and suspended by garters from a belt. In cold weather, men and women wore 'matchcoats' which were cloak-like garments worn draped over the shoulders. . . . Textiles were made from various types of animal fur, grasses and bark, particularly the inner bark of the mulberry tree which produced a fine, pliable cloth similar to linen. . . . Handmade textiles were either dyed with vegetable dyes or painted with mineral paints."

Among the Florida tribes, men wore loincloths made from either deerskin or a cloth of woven palm fronds or pounded roots. Calusa women wore skirts fashioned from woven Spanish moss.

Timucua and Calusa chiefs adorned themselves with elaborate shell belts, painted bird plumes, and copper gorgets (large pendants). Women placed earrings and ear spools made from fish bladders or conch shells in their earlobes. They also wore carved bone hairpins and jewelry made of shell beads, fish teeth, or freshwater pearls. Tattooing, a popular custom among both men and women, was done by pricking the skin with a sharp tool dipped in mineral paint or vegetable dye. Sometimes the entire body from head to toe was decorated in elaborate designs and figures.

Most men of the Southeast shaved the hair off their heads, leaving a tuft on top, although the Choctaw preferred long hair, as did the Timucua, who twisted it into a bun on top of the head. Most of the women wore their hair long and loose. Oils, usually bear fat, were mixed with fragrant herbs and smoothed over the body, giving it a bright sheen as well as a pleasant smell. Most of the people of the Southeast grew fashionably long fingernails.

Spearing was one method of catching fish for the Native Americans of the Southeast, as this Seminole man demonstrates.

Awake, arise, stand up!

It is raising up its head, I believe; I walk about.

Awake, arise, stand up!

It attempts to rise, I believe; I walk about.

Awake, arise, stand up!

Slowly it raises its body, I think; I walk about.

Awake, arise, stand up!

It is now risen to its feet, I presume; I walk about.

Awake, arise, stand up.[10]

Although hunting provided a much-needed source of protein, it was not the only means by which people of the Southeast obtained such nutrients. Fish and seafood were also important protein sources, and along the coastline fishing was even more essential than hunting.

Fishing in a Land of Waterways

Native Americans of the Southeast were skilled fishers, and in southern Florida fishing provided the main staple in the diet. The variety of water bodies in the region made hundreds of different fish and other seafood available to the local people.

From the Mississippi River the Natchez caught catfish and eels. Atlantic sturgeon and other large bottom-dwelling fish were obtained from the tidewater regions. The

Dugout Canoes

The major form of transportation for Native Americans of the Southeast was the dugout canoe, especially in regions where foot travel was difficult, as in the wetlands of southern Florida. Shirley Glubok, in *The Art of the Southeastern Indians,* describes the process of creating a canoe:

"Southeastern Indians made dugout canoes from the long, thick trunks of poplar or cypress trees. A tree was felled by making a fire on the ground around it. The branches were burned off and the bark scraped away with shell tools. The trunk was hollowed out by burning it, bit by bit, and scraping away the ashes with shell or stone tools."

When completed, the long, narrow canoe had a shallow interior and was suited for maneuvering tight waterways. There was a platform at each end on which a person would stand to pole the canoe. Poling was a way of moving the canoe by thrusting a long, thin, wooden pole into shallow water down to the bottom and then pushing against it, over and over. In deeper water six-foot-long wooden paddles were used to propel the canoe.

Two canoes could be tied together, with two poles extending between them. Mats were laid over the poles to form a platform. Such a large catamaran was more stable and could carry much larger loads of fish, game, or trade goods.

Biloxi, Timucua, and Calusa would have found such saltwater fish as mackerel, flounder, and grouper off the seacoast. The Creek, Choctaw, and Chickasaw had freshwater fish like perch and bass available to them.

There were many fishing tools employed, but one of the most common was the weir, a community fish trap set in shallow water. There are several weir designs, but the Southeast tribes used hoop-shaped tubes, which they covered with hides. In addition, fish were often hunted with bow and arrow or with spears. Among the Timucua and Calusa, whose main source of protein was fish and shellfish, fishing was accomplished with the use of nets, spears, and bone hooks, which were not attached to a pole.

Because the Florida tribes lived in a swampy land strewn with meandering waterways, travel on foot could be difficult. As a result, wooden dugout canoes were used to traverse the inland waterways and the ocean. Using a variety of fishing tools, anything from a tiny minnow to a huge whale could be caught.

Gathering the Wild Plants

In addition to fish and seafood, Native Americans of the Southeast gathered many plants from the wild to add variety to their diet. They also gathered plant material to use in making tools, baskets, houses, and many other items. Some plants were valued for their medicinal properties.

In Florida, the Calusa and Timucua gathered wild grapes, persimmons, and prickly pear fruit. The inland people collected nuts such as chestnuts, walnuts, and pecans. They also enjoyed the sweet fruit of wild strawberries, blackberries, and mulberries. Wild plums, cherries, and grapes were also popular throughout the region.

Along the coast of the Gulf of Mexico, wild rice and wild sweet potatoes were available. In Georgia and South Carolina, the Cherokee tapped sugar from maple trees, from which they made maple syrup and maple sugar, both important trade items.

Many rituals and taboos existed regulating the use of plant life. Some important plants, like ginseng, were shown great respect by passing over the first three plants discovered. The fourth was then dug up and collected. In its place a small token such as a bead was placed on the ground as payment. A prayer of thanks similar to that of the hunter was chanted to appease the plant's spirit and encourage its rebirth.

Despite the abundance of edible plants in the southeast region, Native Americans did not depend on the food they gathered for subsistence. Rather, agriculture provided the primary sustenance for the people of the Southeast.

Farming

In the early spring, fields were prepared for planting by burning the underbrush and the crop remains from the year before. The ash that subsequently blanketed the fields provided a rich fertilizer. New fields were cleared by girdling the trees that stood there. Girdling was done by hacking a ring through the bark all around the tree. This left the tree vulnerable to insects and diseases, and it was only a matter of time before the tree weakened and died, making it easily removable.

The men then upturned the soil with hoes made from shell, stone, or bone. Women followed, forming holes in the soil with digging sticks, into which seeds were dropped. Corn seeds were often planted in holes made atop small hand-molded hills.

The most important crop to be planted was corn, of which there were several varieties. Beans were always planted with corn because they returned nutrients to the soil that the corn took. Squash, including pumpkin, was also planted in rows alongside the corn and beans, creating the trio often called the "Three Sisters." By summer the thick tangle of vines and stalks kept weeds from growing and overtaking the field.

Besides the Three Sisters, tobacco, gourds, and sunflowers were also grown. In Florida, the Timucua planted garlic, onion, citron, and different types of melon.

Once the planting was completed, it was the job of the women to tend the

An important food source, corn could be prepared immediately after the harvest or stored for later preparation.

fields through the summer and early autumn. Children chased away crows and small animals that nibbled away at the growing crops.

The first corn crop was harvested in mid- to late summer, while the second was ready in midautumn. The corn stalks were cut and then the ears either prepared in some manner or placed in a communal storehouse maintained in case of lean

times. In some years one or both crops would be destroyed by drought, floods, or early frost, and unusually long, harsh winters could leave a tribe nearly starving by spring as the previous year's corn supply dwindled.

Food Preparation and Storage

After the harvest and the fall hunting expeditions, the preparation of meats and plant food took a great deal of time for the Native American women of the Southeast. In 1775 historian Bernard Romans described Creek food in his book *A Concise Natural History of East and West Florida:* "They make pancakes; they dry the tongues of their venison . . . they eat much roasted and broiled venison, a great deal of milk and eggs . . . also dried peaches and persimmons and other fruits and berries, as well as their particular boast, a prepared drink known as 'hickory milk'. . . . In a word, they have the greatest abundance available."[11]

According to Romans, the Creek prepared corn in forty-two different ways. It could be roasted on the cob, or slow-boiled with turkey and lye to make a favorite dish called *sagamite*. It was combined with beans or other vegetables to make a stew. A favorite pastime was to toss an ear of corn into a fire and catch the

Native American Basketry

Native American women of the Southeast were highly skilled basket makers. Baskets were made from river cane that was split into long, narrow strips, trimmed, and scraped till smooth. Then the strips were soaked in vegetable dyes, such as black obtained from the black walnut, deep brown from the butternut, red or orange from puccoon root, and yellow from yellowroot.

The strips were then woven in a checkerboard pattern of regular over and under turns. Twilling—varying the width and color of splints and the number of overlapping turns—could create intricate designs.

Cherokee women were well known for their basketry, and often used geometric designs such as squares, triangles, and crosses over the whole basket. The Chitimacha, who lived in southern Louisiana, were known for weaving colorful bands of designs that curved over the entire basket.

Most Native American women of the Southeast made baskets for the purpose of storing or collecting food. Some baskets were woven loosely to be used as sieves. They also wove baskets with handles and articles such as sitting or sleeping mats, hampers, and decorative wall hangings. One of the most distinctive creations was the burden basket, a large, tightly woven basket with a flared opening. It could be carried on the back or head for use in the fields.

Seminole women made "sweetgrass" baskets from a wild grass that grew in the higher areas of the Everglades where the ground stayed dry. The sweetgrass was washed and laid out to dry in the sun. The blades were then sewn together with colorful threads and woven into baskets of various shapes.

A Cherokee woman weaves a basket accented by decorative bands.

popped corn that exploded out of it. One of the most popular corn dishes was hominy, still enjoyed in many parts of the United States today. To make hominy, dried kernels were pounded to remove the husks. The cracked pieces of corn, called grits, were then boiled for several hours in lye water.

Cooking with lye was a common preparation used by Native Americans of the Southeast for many corn dishes in addition to hominy. A small amount of lye was combined with corn and any other desired ingredients in a large pot of water, and boiled for anywhere from half an hour to several hours depending on the dish. The corn mixture was then repeatedly washed with clean water until all the deadly lye was gone. An important nutritional aid, the lye increased the amount of useable nutrients like protein and vitamin B that otherwise would remain locked inside the kernel.

Other crops and gathered plants were made into special dishes as well. Adair commented on the menus of the southeastern peoples: "It is surprising to see the great variety of dishes they make out of wild flesh, corn, beans, peas, potatoes, pompions (pumpkins), dried fruits, herbs, and roots. They can diversify their courses, as much as the English, or perhaps the French cooks: and in either of the ways they dress their food, it is grateful to a wholesome stomach."[12]

Berries and other fruits were usually dried or stewed so they would keep for long periods. Nuts were parched to extract their oil. They could also be ground up and boiled, and then the oil strained out through a cloth. The remainder of the nut was thrown away. Nut oil was a delicious seasoning for corn, vegetables, or meat dishes.

Meat was sun-dried and then smoked, or it could be stretched out on a rack and dried over a fire. The dried meats would keep through the long winter when fresh meat from hunting was not available. Venison, the most common meat, was roasted or broiled. Meat was also stewed with vegetables or barbecued for a delicious flavor.

A great deal of daily life involved the acquiring or cultivation of food, and its preparation and related activities formed a central element in the spiritual beliefs and practices of Native Americans of the Southeast.

Chapter 4

Keeping the Balance

Native Americans of the Southeast believed that the universe was characterized by oppositions: upper versus lower and good versus evil. Such opposing relationships could be kept in balance only when harmony between the entities was maintained. The people sought this ideal of harmony, which gave order and meaning to a physical universe that often seemed to be trying to kill them, by investing all their actions with spirituality. At the core of each task there had to be respect for the earth, and for the human spirit and body.

The spiritual practices of the people of the Southeast seem to have evolved from the sun worship of their Mississippian forebears. The sun, the center of the universe, was seen as the source of life and sustenance, giving warmth and light so that living things could survive on earth. Some tribes had a special name for the sun deity. The Choctaw called this supreme being *Hashtahli*, meaning "sun"

and "to complete the action." The Natchez believed the sun lived on earth in the form of their leader, the Great Sun. In keeping with this theme, the sacred fire that burned in the central plaza of most southeastern Native American towns was regarded as a form of the sun on earth. Similarly, there was a fire at the center of every unit, including each individual household.

In addition to the sun deity, the people of the southeast believed in many other spirits and lesser deities, whose opposing relationships dictated numerous daily practices and gave them a spiritual basis.

Spirits of Good and Evil

Rather than a lord of evil like Satan of the Judeo-Christian traditions, Native Americans of the Southeast believed in several lesser spirits who embodied evil. In addition, there were many good spirits who countered the effects of the bad.

The Legend of Strawberries

The legend of the strawberries is a Cherokee story that teaches people to set differences aside. This version is retold in James Mooney's *History, Myths and Sacred Formulas of the Cherokees:*

"When the first man was created and a mate was given to him, they lived together very happily for a time, but then began to quarrel, until at last the woman left her husband and started off toward . . . the east. The man followed alone and grieving, but the woman kept on steadily ahead and never looked behind, until 'Unelanunhi,' . . . (The Sun), took pity on him and asked him if he was still angry with his wife. He said he was not, and 'Unelanunhi' then asked him if he would like to have her back again, to which he eagerly answered yes.

So 'Unelanunhi' caused a patch of the finest ripe huckleberries to spring up along the path in front of the woman, but she passed by without paying any attention to them. Farther on he put a clump of blackberries, but these also she refused to notice . . . [S]he . . . went on until suddenly she saw in front a patch of large ripe strawberries, the first ever known. She stooped to gather a few to eat, and as she picked them . . . the memory of her husband came back to her and she found herself unable to go on. She sat down, but the longer she waited the stronger became her desire for her husband, and at last she gathered a bunch of the finest berries and started back along the path to give them to him. He met her kindly and they went home together."

Protection from evil spirits was sought in the form of a totem, which served as a guide or guardian angel. A person was thought to absorb the strengths and other attributes of his or her totem. Often a piece of the totem, such as a bone or piece of hide, was held in a medicine bag worn around the neck. The medicine bag could also hold other personal items that would give the wearer power, wisdom, or strength. Such items as minerals, bones, dirt, hair, or plants could bring good fortune or ward off evil. During the early nineteenth century, Indian agent Benjamin Hawkins noted that the Creek kept in their medicine bags "a charm, a protection against all ills, called the war physic, composed of . . . bones of the snake and [mountain] lion."[13] Indeed, bone fragments of mountain lions or other fierce predators were a common addition to medicine bags, as the wearer believed he or she would then absorb the power and cunning of this animal. Many of these totem spirits played roles in tribal legends and myths.

How Legends Kept Law and Order

Native Americans kept a tradition of telling the oral history of the tribe as well as stories such as fables and legends. Such stories helped to pass on customs and social mores to generation after generation. Legends educated people about law and culture and established a tribal identity.

The religion of the people of the Southeast as expressed in stories was directly related to tribal law and morality. Historical writer Carolyn Keller Reeves explains this:

> The different types of stories served to maintain different aspects of Choctaw society. Legends imparted knowledge of Choctaw history, manner of government, and responsibilities, the discharge of which ensured the well being of the people. Myths provided spiritual explanations for the existence of environmental phenomena, which could not otherwise be understood. The fables helped regulate social behavior by giving instruction regarding the consequences of unrestrained actions.[14]

Native Americans of the Southeast depended on a strict following of customs and rituals in order to maintain the balance between the needs of the earth and their own needs. Susan DePrim, a legal historian, concludes that "the . . . environmental morality functioning as their prevailing religion seems to provide a strong foundation for their legal system, which stressed respect for the individual and the environment and punitive measures which would restore the 'balance of the universe.'"[15]

Medicine Men of the Southeast Tribes

The principal spiritual leader and healer of a town was the medicine man, who came

A medicine man with his patient. The medicine man was both healer and spiritualist.

to his position after many years of training, often after having revealed a talent for spiritual matters or healing as a child. His observances and warnings carried great weight in the community, influencing how people lived, where a new town would be built, or whether to go to war.

Medicine to the Native American was more than just a pill or tonic to make a person feel better. It was more universal, as described by a cultural historian:

> [Indian medicine consisted of] clairvoyance [foreknowledge], ecstaism [trancelike rapture], spiritism, divination, demonology, prophesy, necromancy [magic used to communicate with the dead], and all things incomprehensible. Hence, the medicine man is not only the primitive doctor, but he is the diviner, the rain-maker, the soothsayer, the prophet, the priest, and in some instances, the chief or king.[16]

In addition to presiding over seasonal ceremonies, the medicine man was also called by families to be present at births and deaths.

The healing power of the medicine man was believed to stem from his ability to recognize many disease-causing spirits that could possess poisonous plants or roots, or could be embodied by witches. It was his responsibility to discover which spirit was causing a given ailment and then prescribe the standard treatment, of which there was one for every bad spirit known.

A medicine man followed a series of steps in diagnosing a disease. When a person came to him complaining of ill health, he first asked where the pain, if any, was located. He followed this inquiry with questions about whether the person had broken any taboos, seen any omens, or had any dreams.

After thoroughly interviewing the patient, the medicine man would suggest possible causes that fit the symptoms. If the questioning failed to suggest a likely cause, the medicine man would invoke the help of spirits in seeking the source of the ailment.

Once the cause was known, curing could take place. The cure might be as simple as following the dictate of an omen or fulfilling a desire as revealed in a dream. If a physical cause was found, the medicine man would gather the appropriate herbs and roots and make a concoction to give to the patient.

Whatever remedy was given, it was followed by singing or chanting of magical formulas to threaten the disease-causing spirit with a rival spirit. If the medicine man was successful, the bad spirit would be driven away, allowing the patient to regain good health. A chant for the treatment of headache or dizziness appears in *Indians of the Southeast:*

> Gallop away
>
> Gallop away
>
> Gallop away
>
> Red rat

Red cloud

My head

Is hot

Is roaring.[17]

Probably the most important factor in the effectiveness of a cure was the emotional mindset established by a combination of faith in the medicine man as a healer and belief that the chants and other remedies would undoubtedly lead to a cure.

Herbal Remedies

Medicine men were familiar with many wild roots and herbs that they collected for healing. James Adair praised the skill of Native Americans in healing, claiming "they . . . have a great knowledge of specific virtues in simples [medicinal plants]; applying herbs and plants, on the most dangerous occasions, and seldom if ever fail to effect a thorough cure, from the natural bush."[18]

Herbs were usually boiled in water and then either applied to the skin, rubbed into lacerations, or blown over the patient through a cane tube. They were also steeped to produce a medicinal tea.

One common plant used was the willow tree. Its bark was used to reduce swelling and nosebleeds. Consumed as a tea it cured headaches, reduced fevers, and relieved aches. Today we know that willow

Sweat lodges were used to restore health and rid the body of impurities.

contains salicin, a fever and pain reducer used in aspirin.

Corn was also of great value in curing. The smoke from burning corncobs was used to relieve itching skin. Cornmeal mixed with water was poured over the head of a person with a fever. Today cornstarch is a well-known folk remedy for chapped, irritated skin.

The Sweat Lodge

Perhaps the most renowned way of healing developed by Native Americans was the

The Origin of Corn

Since corn was the major life-giving food of the people of the Southeast, many stories evolved that explained how this important plant came to them. One version is retold in John R. Swanton's *Source Material for the Social and Ceremonial Life of the Choctaw Indians:*

"The two hunters, having been unsuccessful in the chase of that. . . day, found themselves on that night with nothing with which to satisfy the cravings of hunger except a black hawk. . . .

They cooked the hawk and sat down to partake of their . . . supper, when their attention was drawn . . . by the low but distinct tones, strange yet soft and plaintive as the melancholy notes of the dove. . . .

[T]hey looked up and down the river to learn whence the sounds proceeded. . . . But happening to look behind them in the direction opposite the moon they saw a woman of wonderful beauty standing upon a mound. . . . She beckoned them to approach, while she seemed surrounded by a halo of light that gave her a supernatural appearance. . . .

At once they approached (the spot) where she stood, and offered their assistance. . . . She replied she was very hungry, whereupon one of them ran and brought the roasted hawk and handed it to her. She accepted it with grateful thanks; but after eating a small portion of it, she handed the remainder back to them replying that she would remember their kindness when she returned to her home in the happy hunting grounds of her father. . . . She then told them that when the next mid-summer moon should come they must meet her at the mound upon which she was then standing.

She then . . . disappeared. The two hunters returned to their camp for the night and early next morning sought their homes. . . . The mid-summer full moon found the two hunters at the foot of the mound but (the woman) was nowhere to be seen. Then remembering she had told them they must come to the very spot where she was then standing, they at once ascended the mound and found it covered with a strange plant, which yielded an excellent food, which was ever afterwards cultivated by the Choctaws, and named by them Tunchi (corn)."

sweat lodge. Not only was heavy sweating considered very effective in curing certain ailments like arthritis or rheumatism, it could serve to purify the body, as well.

The sweat lodge was a small hut covered with bark or animal skins. Inside, the floor was covered with hot stones, over which pots of steaming water were continuously poured. Often herbs were also placed inside the lodge so that their healing effects would rise with the steam to be taken in by the body.

Inside the lodge, a person would sit on a board together with several other people who chanted or sang until they were heavily perspiring. Writing of his visit with the Indians of the region in 1753, French trader Jean Bernard Bossu described the lodges of the Choctaw as "steam cabinets in which . . . [t]he vapor filled with the essence and salts of these herbs enters the patient's body through his pores and his nose and restores his strength."[19] After sweating for a while, a person would leave the lodge, run to the nearest stream, and jump in to allow the cold water to wash away the impurities of the body that had come to the surface with the sweat. Both men and women commonly underwent such purification before important ceremonies or events.

Rituals and Ceremonies

Native Americans of the Southeast expressed their joy and respect for the gifts of the earth through seasonal ceremonies that were both festive and solemn, and always involved song and dance. The purpose of the ceremony was to ensure the continued balance and harmony between nature and the people by giving thanks and respect to the earth in return for enjoying her bounty.

Native Americans believed that part of showing respect for the earth was making the body pure before engaging in a spiritual activity. Purity of body led to purity of mind, and clear thinking was essential when one was bargaining with nature for the future sustenance of the people. Thus ceremonies that included rituals of purification and self-renewal were enacted many times over the course of a year.

One purification rite was called "going to water." The person to be cleansed stood in a river and endured three hundred scratches from a comb set with seven rattlesnake teeth. Upon completion of the scratching, the person turned to face the east and washed the blood from his body. While doing so he chanted a prayer for success in a future undertaking, such as a hunt or a game.

The Black Drink

The most popular purification ritual was partaking of the Black Drink, an observance universally made by Native Americans of the Southeast. The Creek called it *asi*, a strong tea brewed from a variety of holly. One traveler among the tribes of the Southeast prior to the eighteenth century commented on their use of the tea, "[which they drank in large quantities,] vomiting it up again as clear [soon] as they drink it. Besides their great Dieretick Quality their Tea carries off a great deal that perhaps might prejudice their Health by Agues and Fevers."[20] The powerful effect of vomiting and perspiration from drinking the hot tea led the Native Americans to believe the Black Drink was a gift from the Great Spirit. It was believed to cleanse the body and mind of

Native American Music and Dance

Almost all native dances were characterized by slow, shuffling steps. A common ceremonial dance was the corn dance, while some social dances were the friendship dance and the war dance. An animal dance such as the fox dance may have been a ritual to call the fox before embarking on a hunting trip. Burt and Ferguson, in *Indians of the Southeast,* describe a friendship dance:

"Around a night camp fire young, unmarried men would form a ring about an inner ring of young, unmarried women. The men would then move in a circle simulating the course of the sun, the females moved in the opposite direction. As they did the slow, shuffling step the men would strike their arms with their open hands. The girls would follow, clapping their hands, and, in [eighteenth-century botanist William] Bartram's phrase, 'raise their shrill sweet voices, answering an elevated shout of the men at stated times.'"

The music for dances was created from a variety of instruments, including wooden drums, gourd rattles, and tortoiseshell rattles. Flutes made from bone or reed were popular also, but seem to have been used more for personal enjoyment rather than official events.

Songs always accompanied the dance. Songs that spoke of a moral principle were popular, as were those that prayed for success in some future endeavor, such as a hunt, war raid, or stickball game.

A Choctaw dancer wears an elaborately decorated costume and a feathered headdress.

impurities, and to provide a person with stamina and clear thinking.

The Black Drink was most often consumed before war raids, hunting expeditions, stickball games, and spiritual ceremonies. It was also drunk prior to important council meetings and coming-of-age ceremonies for males.

Death Rituals of the Southeast Tribes

The death customs of the people of the Southeast were extremely elaborate. The respect they held for the bones of their ancestors is evident in the funeral process, described by writer and historian Len Green regarding the Choctaw:

> Upon death, the body of the Choctaw was placed on a platform raised above the ground . . . out in the clear enough that the breezes could pass on all sides of the body to help with the "ripening." Generally, one moon month (28 days) was allowed for the body to become decomposed enough so that the Bonepicker could perform his part of the ceremony. While the body was "ripening," the family of the dead person prepared for the final ceremony. . . .
>
> Relatives and friends would bring extra food for the funeral feast, and while the food was being prepared, the Bonepicker performed his services. He built a large fire, removing the flesh from the bones of the dead and destroying it in the flames.

> With his long, tough fingernails he removed all bits of decayed flesh, gristle and tendon from each bone and scraped it smooth. When all of the bones had been cleaned, they were placed into either a bag made from animal skins or into a basket woven tightly from bamboo cane with a lid that fastened tightly. When the Bonepicker's job was completed, the family then invited relatives and friends to partake of a funeral feast in memory of the departed.

> Following the feast, the bones were taken to the "bone house". . . . And here the bones remained until the time of the "Festival of Mourning for the Dead." When the "Festival" time arrived, each family collected its bones from the bone house and transported them to the sacred mound. The mound was opened, the bones were placed inside and the mound again closed. After all the bones had been placed, the Festival of Mourning for the Dead was staged with feasting and religious dancing.[21]

The Bonepickers, who enjoyed very high status, grew their fingernails extremely long for use in their grisly job. They were distinctively tattooed so that everyone knew who they were.

The family always placed the dead person's medicine bag, food (usually corn), drink, clothing, and utensils with the body for the spirit's use in his or her journey to the afterworld.

Every spiritual custom and religious ceremony served one chief purpose for the native people of the Southeast—to maintain harmony and balance in the world. Taking and giving, and good and evil, were factors that must be kept on an equal footing, lest one gain power over the other. In the years to come this crucial balance would be threatened, endangering the world of the Native American.

Chapter 5

European Contact and Cultural Decline

For many Native American tribes, the coming of the Europeans meant instant cultural annihilation, while for others the destruction was a slow and gradual process of pecking away at tribal customs and lands. Stories of how white strangers had lied to and enslaved people in the Caribbean may have reached the tribes living in southern Florida as early as 1512.

In the spring of 1513 a Spanish explorer named Juan Ponce de León landed on the eastern coast of Florida. When Ponce de León and his men met the Calusa, the chief was suspicious of their motives but feigned interest in the avowals of friendship offered to his people. Hoping to encourage the foreigners to look elsewhere for friends, the Calusa launched a surprise attack on the Spaniards. But Ponce de León did not give up easily; he sent an envoy to negotiate peace with the Calusa. The chief returned with eighty canoes of armed warriors and fought for nearly twelve hours. In the end, the Spanish left without the gold and slaves they were seeking. Eight years later, Ponce de León returned to southern Florida, and once again the Calusa battled his troops.

A 1728 portrait of the sixteenth-century Spanish explorer Juan Ponce de León.

During one of the skirmishes, Ponce de León was struck by an arrow and mortally wounded. It would be two decades before the Spanish returned to Florida.

De Soto's Journey of Terror

Hernando de Soto was a conquistador, or explorer, with a mission to enrich Spain by acquiring land and gold in the New World. De Soto arrived in Florida in 1539 with six hundred armed men and several missionaries to explore the southeast region in search of a legendary city of gold. His massive entourage sparked curiosity among the local peoples. The chief of the Ichisi, a small southeastern tribe, remarked: "Think, then, what must be the effect of the sight of you and your people, whom we have at no time seen, astride the fierce brutes, your horses, entering with such speed and fury into my country . . . things altogether new, as to strike awe and terror into our hearts."[22] There were over two hundred horses, and three hundred hogs; one hundred African and Native American slaves carried the provisions.

De Soto swept through Native American towns like a tornado, ransacking villages, destroying burial sites, stealing food and supplies, and enslaving the people. He and

Spanish conquistador Hernando de Soto arrives at the Mississippi River. De Soto traveled across the Southeast looking for the fabled city of gold.

The Story of Tuscaloosa

In October 1540 Hernando de Soto's entourage arrived in the territory of the Choctaw chief Tuscaloosa. Although suspicious of the Europeans, Tuscaloosa received them with a great show of power, riches, and grandeur.

De Soto requested that the Choctaw provide him with four hundred bearers and a hundred women for his journey. Tuscaloosa, however, had a plan. He graciously agreed to provide the requested persons, but informed the Spaniards that they would be waiting at the next town, Mabila. He would send a runner ahead to organize the group.

The unsuspecting Spaniards set off for Mabila, but when they arrived they found the town heavily palisaded. As the Spanish soldiers entered the town plaza Choctaw warriors ambushed them, and a battle raged for several hours. Thousands of Choctaw, armed with clubs and bows and arrows, died in the fight against men with guns and swords, but de Soto's men also suffered heavy losses: their horses had been slaughtered and their supplies destroyed. Only forty soldiers were killed, but almost all the survivors had been wounded. The Europeans dragged themselves across the land, continuously ambushed by small groups of Chickasaw. Tuscaloosa had succeeded in so damaging the Spaniards that for the rest of the journey, de Soto's expedition never regained its strength.

his men progressed north through Florida and into Georgia and the Carolinas, where he encountered the Timucua and the Creek. One Florida chief is reputed to have said, "I have long since learned who you Castilians are. . . . To me you are professional vagabonds who wander from place to place, gaining your livelihood by robbing, sacking, and murdering people who have given you no offense."[23]

In May 1540 de Soto met the Cherokee while crossing the Blue Ridge Mountains. Fortunately, he treated the Cherokee with respect, and there were no recorded conflicts with them, although many small Cherokee towns apparently were deserted when de Soto came upon them. After coming down out of the mountains, he once again crossed paths with the Creek. In the Alabama region de Soto met the Choctaw, who did not trust the Spaniards. A battle raged between the two peoples that determined the fate of the rest of the journey for de Soto's men. On the Mississippi-Alabama border the conquistadors encountered the fierce Chickasaw, who continuously harassed the Spaniards with hit-and-run attacks.

Wounded and short of supplies, the Spaniards returned to the Mississippi

River in 1542, where de Soto and many of his men died of an illness not known to European medicine. In the summer of 1543 the surviving Spaniards sailed down the Mississippi toward the Gulf of Mexico and into Spanish territory. According to one report, along the way a native shouted after the Spaniards, "If we possessed such large canoes, we would follow you to your land and conquer it, for we too are men."[24] To the Europeans, de Soto's expedition had been a dismal failure, but to the Native Americans of the Southeast it had been a meeting with terror.

The Fate of the Timucua and the Calusa

Despite their resistance half a century earlier, both the Timucua and the Calusa were among the first tribes to succumb to the Europeans. After the Spaniards established the town of St. Augustine in Florida in 1565, the first permanent European settlement in North America, Native Americans were converted to Christianity largely through the efforts of Roman Catholic missionaries who lived and worked among the tribes.

The Calusa also allowed a Spanish garrison to be built near their main town. However, in 1569, tragedy struck the tribe: as punishment for conspiring against the Spanish, the town's chief and several councilmen were put to death. In revenge, the Calusa burned the garrison. Then they went into hiding in the woods. Many Calusa eventually assimilated into other tribes farther north.

The northern tribes were not always friendly, however. Up the Atlantic coast, the English had successfully established a colony at Jamestown, Virginia, in 1607. In less than a hundred years the English had enlisted the aid of Creek and Yuchi warriors in raiding Florida in an effort to drive out the Spanish. Frequent brutal attacks often extended from Spanish settlements to neighboring Native American towns. These raids destroyed over thirty-two Timucua towns and Spanish missions.

Over time, the population of the Timucua dwindled from disease, and many died as victims of war or slavery. The remaining Calusa suffered the same results. Many tiny remnants of both tribes survived in Florida until the eighteenth century, when they were joined by Creek refugees from the north and evolved into the modern Seminole tribe.

The Fall of the Catawba

With the founding of Jamestown, the English became the northern neighbors of the Catawba in South Carolina. Initially, a good trade relationship caused the Catawba to ally themselves with the colonists. Over the years, however, the continued enslavement of Native Americans fueled the anger of the Catawba, and in 1715 they united with the Yamasee to fight the English. The war was short but cost the Native Americans dearly. Thousands of Catawba were killed before peace was reestablished later that same year.

Alcoholism

From the earliest days of European trade, white traders gave Native Americans alcohol, usually rum or whiskey, to make them easier to take advantage of in negotiations. Native Americans had no experience with fermented drinks and thus had no custom of social drinking, so when offered alcohol they often drank to the point of intoxication.

Warriors thought alcohol made them more courageous, while medicine men imagined that it increased their spiritual powers. Many natives developed serious addictions, which made them dependent on the whims of the European traders who supplied the liquor. Some men would trade a whole year's worth of hides for one jug of rum, while others sold wives and children into slavery for the drink.

Health and criminal problems multiplied in some communities where more than half the population had drinking problems. Some people got so drunk they fell into fires and burned to death, or fell to their deaths from cliffs. Brawls and murders became common, and the traditional revenge system was forgotten as intoxicated natives took matters into their own hands rather than allowing the clan to exact retribution.

Desperate Native American leaders who attempted to end the problem by pleading with white traders to cease the liquor trade often received death threats from their warriors, who were unwilling to stop drinking. Although white traders agreed to curtail the liquor trade, it was so profitable that the promise was never honored. According to the Editors of Reader's Digest, in *Through Indian Eyes*, a Catawba chief known as King Haglar bemoaned the state of his people in 1757, saying, "You sell it to our young men, and give it to them, many times . . . it rots their guts and causes our men to get very sick, and many of our people have lately died by the effects, and I heartily wish you would do something to prevent your people from daring to sell or give them any of that strong drink."

A white trader offers a Native American a bottle of alcohol.

The remainder of the eighteenth century brought the gradual destruction of the Catawba. Their numbers steadily plummeted as hundreds died from disease and alcoholism, and many others were killed by raiding Shawnee and Iroquois from the north. By 1775, there were only four hundred Catawba left of the five-thousand-strong nation of just sixty years before.

The Fall of the Natchez

Prior to 1729 the Natchez had traded peacefully with the French, but conflict erupted that year when the French demanded that the Natchez abandon their principal town to allow the French governor to construct a house on the site. The Natchez had no intention of leaving. The French did not understand that the home of the Great Sun was a sacred site, as were the town's burial mounds. No foreigner could just walk onto their land and demand that their god-king move out of the way.

Tensions mounted on both sides, and in the fall of 1729 the Natchez attacked the French, killing two hundred of them. The Natchez settled back into their daily routine, confident that the French had been thwarted. For a while there was peace, but two years later the French struck back, their large army augmented by Choctaw and other Native Americans who regarded the Natchez as the enemy. The tragic end is described in *Through Indian Eyes*:

For the Natchez it was a cataclysm: More than 1,000 men, women, and children died defending the Great Sun—and French slave traders took almost 500 others to sell to merchants in the Caribbean. Natchez prisoners deemed unfit for slavery were tortured or burned. Those who survived fled the region and sought refuge in Cherokee and other native communities. With a persistence shown again and again by displaced tribal groups, the refugees managed to preserve aspects of their culture in new surroundings—even continuing to use the Natchez language for several generations. But the ancient and majestic Natchez kingdom itself, at the whim of an alien empire, had in the span of a few years been extinguished forever.[25]

Early Alliances Between Europeans and the Southeast Tribes

Although many tribes suffered grave injustices at the hands of Europeans, the explorers and colonists did attempt to maintain peaceful relations with some native peoples. The Spanish in Florida, the English on the Atlantic coast, and the French along the Mississippi and on the Gulf coast each attempted to enlist the support of particular tribes in driving out their competitors. Such support was often gained through trade relationships and by pitting one tribe against its traditional enemies.

Being located between the three European factions, the Creek were in the most precarious situation of all the tribes; but they were very skilled diplomats who used this position to play one group against another for their own benefit. Largely for geographical reasons, the Choctaw traded and allied themselves with the French, while the Chickasaw supported the English. The Cherokee maintained good relations with both the French and English. Indeed, in the territory north of Florida, the French and the English were the only Europeans the Native Americans had for trading partners.

European Trade

Until the establishment of Charleston in South Carolina in 1670, most trading was conducted with the French. After 1670, English traders traveled among the Creek, Choctaw, Chickasaw, and Cherokee, and Charleston became a bustling

Slavery

Thousands of Native Americans were captured and made to labor as slaves alongside Africans in North America. Europeans considered them to be a valuable resource for providing the labor needed to operate New England tobacco fields and southern cotton plantations. Many were also auctioned and shipped out of Charleston to work on Caribbean sugar plantations.

Europeans used a variety of means to capture and enslave the people of the Southeast. In the aftermath of a fight, Native American survivors were rounded up and forced into slavery. Whites encouraged intertribal warfare and the capture of prisoners who could be exchanged for European trade goods. During the sixteenth and seventeenth centuries it was a common practice to lure unsuspecting natives on board a ship and then suddenly raise anchor and sail away with the group of bewildered captives. Sometimes peaceful towns were raided entirely for the purpose of securing slaves, especially among the Christianized tribes of northern Florida, where nearly twelve thousand had been auctioned into slavery by 1710.

The fates of Native American slaves were very similar to those of African slaves. For those who were sent to islands in the Caribbean, escape was nearly impossible, but some did manage to flee the tobacco fields and cotton plantations and return to their homes. However, most lived out their lives as slaves. By the time the Emancipation Proclamation became law in 1863, very few Native Americans remained in slavery, as the population had died out. Those who lived within the jurisdiction of the United States were freed along with the African slaves and their descendants, but few reassimilated with their people; by then many generations had passed, and hereditary ties had all but vanished.

Animals such as deer, beaver, and bison (pictured) were hunted more extensively as the European demand for skins rose.

hub of commerce between colonists and native peoples.

Europeans traded their wares mostly for the tanned skins of the white-tailed deer. They also took beaver, bear, and even bison, but deerskin was especially valued in Europe, where it was used for fine gloves, bookbindings, and other leather goods. In the 1750s alone over 150,000 skins were shipped from Charleston to Europe each year. Hunting on a massive scale to meet market demands was contrary to the Native Americans' traditional beliefs about killing animals. Soon, however, the hunters abandoned the practice of thanking the spirits of the animals they killed, a tacit admis-

sion that they were no longer trying simply to provide food and clothing for their families.

But if the Native Americans yielded to European pressure to keep up the supply of skins and furs, they insisted that trade customs be strictly adhered to. When word of an approaching trader came, warriors were sent to greet him and ensure that he came in peace. The trader was offered a meal and lodging. Prior to trade negotiations, the chief and head councilmen expected to receive gifts such as earrings, brass belt buckles, glass mirrors, or jewelry. The actual trading took place according to certain rules of etiquette. A trader was required to eat heartily, speak softly, avoid staring, and act calmly. To do otherwise was considered rude behavior and brought on the wrath of the chief, who consequently stopped the trade and sent the offender away.

Native Americans coveted European goods mainly because they made life easier. Metal utensils and tools did not crack and lasted longer than wood. Acquiring manufactured cloth eliminated the time-consuming tasks of tanning hides or weaving cane to make clothing or bedding. Glass and metal trinkets, which were considered exotic and valuable, appealed to their appreciation of beauty and adornment. Other items traded included needles, fishhooks, spun thread, blankets, and coarse, colored cloth. Native Americans were fascinated by mirrors and loved to collect tiny glass beads. The men bartered for knives, hatchets, and, significantly, guns and ammunition.

Unfortunately, southeastern peoples became increasingly dependent on trade goods for subsistence, in turn making them dependent on the Europeans who provided them. Women stopped making pottery and baskets and instead used metal pots. As the traditional ways of doing things were set aside and not taught to younger generations, they began to be forgotten. A writer and painter, William Byrd, wrote in 1728, "Bows and Arrows are grown into disuse except only

Bad Credit

There were a number of unscrupulous white traders who looked upon Native American ignorance of European customs as an easy moneymaking venture. The notion of credit, or borrowing with the intention of paying later, was alien to the people of the Southeast, so when traders offered them goods in exchange for hides to be delivered later it seemed to the Native Americans that they were getting an unbelievably good deal.

Unfortunately, the people of the Southeast were not aware of the outrageous prices and high interest being charged them. A passage by the Editors of Reader's Digest in *Through Indian Eyes* portrays the situation that soon developed: "Credit turned quickly to debt, and eventually, no matter how hard they hunted, many Indians had little hope of ever clearing their ledgers. It is said that early in the 18th century the Yamasee tribe of South Carolina ended up owing their Carolina creditors some 100,000 deerskins—a debt that would have taken four years of hunting to repay."

amongst their Boys. Nor is it ill Policy but on the contrary very prudent, thus to furnish the Indians with Fire-Arms, because it makes them depend entirely upon the English, not only for their Trade, but even for their subsistence."[26] As the old ways were set aside, the philosophies that defined the meaning of life for the native peoples were also abandoned and resulted in the gradual erosion of Native American cultural identities.

In spite of the pitfalls of European trade, the people of the Southeast used these trade alliances to build a force against a common threat—the advance of American colonists on North American lands, including the ancestral homelands of Native Americans.

Native Americans in the American Revolution

During the American Revolution in the 1770s and 1780s, both the Cherokee and the Creek allied themselves with the British, hoping to drive out the land-hungry American colonists. Their reasoning was captured by a young Virginia officer named Henry Timberlake:

When Europeans began selling arms to the Native Americans of the Southeast, traditional weapons such as the bow and arrow fell into disuse.

[The colonists] are now so nigh, and encroached daily so far upon them [the Native Americans], that they not only felt the bad effects of it in their hunting grounds, which were spoiled, but had all the reason in the world to apprehend being swallowed up by so potent neighbors or driven from the country inhabited by their fathers, in which they were born and [brought] up, in fine, their native soil, for which all men have a particular tenderness and affection.[27]

The Chickasaw, however, who had earlier supported the British, fought on the side of the colonists, while the Choctaw tried to remain neutral. When American victory became assured, the people of the Southeast were forced to seek a way to coexist peacefully with the new nation. In the future this meant agreeing to treaties that were greatly to their disadvantage. Some were unfair as written, and others, while equitable in their provisions, were unfair in practice because measures designed for the Native Americans' protection were not enforced.

Chapter 6

Dispossession: Difficult Years

By the end of the eighteenth century the new United States of America controlled the eastern part of North America. Because the tribes of the Southeast inhabited much of the new nation, the Americans sought to disenfranchise them through a succession of treaties over a period of fifty years. They wanted the land, and began to call on the state and federal governments to move the Native Americans off the land and open it for settlement by whites.

This policy of Indian removal, which was to prove disastrous for nearly one hundred thousand Native Americans, was sanctioned largely because of assumptions made by a great many whites at the time: that all Indians were uncivilized and uneducated, and were capable only of unorganized roaming and hunting for subsistence. Therefore, the land ought to be settled by civilized persons who were capable of improving the land by farming it.

The overwhelming greed of white settlers propelled them to settle on Native American lands despite the existence from colonial times of treaties stating that the land was the natives' territory and was to remain so forever. When angry Native Americans attacked an illegal settlement, the settlers complained bitterly to the government, which obligingly drew up yet another treaty granting the disputed settlement to the whites and setting "forever" a new boundary between the two peoples. This happened time after time. Usually such treaties called for a land cession in exchange for a sum of money far below the market value of the land at that time.

The Five Civilized Tribes

The people of the Southeast tried a variety of means to make the United States honor the treaties. Their primary strategy was to adopt the European lifestyle because they believed it was the only way to convince the United States to allow them to keep their ancestral lands. By the turn of the nineteenth century, some of the first Native Americans to adopt European customs as their own had become known as

Sequoyah and the Cherokee Alphabet

Sequoyah was born in 1776, the son of Nathaniel Gist, a fur trader, and Wutteh, the daughter of a Cherokee chief. He grew up among the Cherokee and became a silversmith. He first began to consider the idea of a way to write the Cherokee language in 1809 after a white friend showed him how to sign his name in English on his silverwork.

Like Chief William McIntosh, Sequoyah fought at the Battle of Horseshoe Bend alongside Jackson's troops. It was during this time that he realized the significance of having a written language. He saw that white soldiers could send letters home and receive them, read military orders, and record events, but the Cherokee could not. After the war he focused on developing a written code for the Cherokee language.

The first prototype was pictorial, but the massive number of concepts that needed to be represented did not make it practical. He finally devised a phonetic syllabary based on the eighty-five sounds of the Cherokee language.

Sequoyah presented the syllabary to the Cherokee Council in 1821, and it was immediately adopted as official. In less than a year nearly the entire Cherokee Nation became literate. In 1829 Sequoyah moved to Oklahoma, a decade before the forced removal of his people to the region. Here he worked in mining and politics. He went to Mexico (now Texas) in 1843, possibly to visit family, where he died.

Sequoyah's alphabet, based on the eighty-five sounds of the Cherokee language.

the Five Civilized Tribes. They were the Choctaw, Chickasaw, Creek, Cherokee, and Seminole. The Seminole were not an ancient people. Rather, their members were descendants of groups of mostly Creek refugees who had sought freedom in Florida from the white encroachment of the 1700s; later they joined with remnants of the Calusa and Timucua to evolve an identity of their own.

The Five Tribes welcomed missionaries, who converted hundreds to Christianity and built churches and schools. Farms with livestock, blacksmith shops, and mills were opened. Constitutions were written and governments mirroring that of the U.S. federal government were established.

The Cherokee even adopted syllabary, designed by a tribesman named Sequoyah in 1821. It was the first Native American written language. They also established their own newspaper, the *Cherokee Phoenix*.

But the establishment of churches, schools, and farms failed to make the desired impression on the white settlers. They saw only that Indians lived on the land, and feared that their success in agriculture and business would spell disaster for the whites. If the Native Americans became stronger it would be that much harder to evict them from lands the settlers coveted. Over time, many Native Americans came to the understanding that their land would be taken regardless of what they did. This realization embittered many natives and led to growing tensions between them and the white settlers.

The Red Stick War

Dissension grew also within many tribes, with some continuing to support the white lifestyle and others sanctioning a resistance to European influence and dominance. One of the more aggressive groups was a faction of the Creek tribe known as the Red Stick. This group owed its existence to the influence of Tecumseh, a

Sequoyah devised the first Native American written language in 1821.

Alexander McGillivray

One of the most talented diplomats of the southeastern tribes, Alexander McGillivray, was born in 1759. He was the son of a French-Creek mother of the prestigious Wind clan and a Scottish trader and politician from Georgia. His mother named him Hoboi-hili-miko, "Good Child King," and he was raised among the Creek until the age of fourteen. At this time his father sent him to school in Savannah and Charleston.

During the American Revolution McGillivray supported the British, partly because of apprehension over the Georgia settlers' unconcealed desire for Creek territory. After the American victory, he committed himself to preserving Creek interests against the encroaching United States.

Believing that unity between the Spanish in Florida and the Creek was the best hope for fighting American interests, McGillivray organized a conference at Pensacola for all Native Americans of the Southeast in 1784. There he negotiated a treaty with the Spanish, which stated that Spanish trade goods and protection would be provided in exchange for Creek allegiance and their promise to banish all whites except the Spanish from Creek territory. McGillivray was appointed the "commissary of the Creek nation" and given a salary, which he accepted in order to convince the Spanish that they had bought his allegiance. However, no one ever bought Alexander McGillivray, who in 1793 stated that "Washington himself"

could not bribe him "had he the thirteen United States in his belly." Burt and Ferguson, who quote the Creek leader in *Indians of the Southeast*, observe that persuading foreign authorities that they had his support became McGillivray's most successful diplomatic strategy.

In 1790 McGillivray and several other *miccos* were escorted by wagon train to New York for treaty negotiations. He was treated regally by the Americans, and returned the flattery, inducing them to believe that he was won by their show of affection. He did this not only to soften U.S. authorities but also to provoke concern in the Spanish, who wanted to retain Creek support. When negotiations began, the United States asserted that the land ceded by other *miccos* had to be handed over to Georgia. McGillivray would not agree to this, citing the nonvalidity of such treaties. He was in a difficult position, however, because he knew the Creek people could not continue raiding white settlements, as the cost in lives was becoming too great for their population. He managed to preserve most of the lands, giving up only a minimal amount as stated in the Georgia treaties.

McGillivray's stunning diplomatic career was cut short when he died at the age of thirty-four during a meeting in Spanish Florida, succumbing to the gout and rheumatism that had plagued him most of his life.

Shawnee chief who traveled among the southeastern tribes in 1811, in an attempt to persuade them to join his union of Indian peoples to prevent further settlement on their lands. While the Choctaw and Chickasaw were not convinced, the already dissenting Creek seized the philosophy as their own. In a series of raids now known as the Red Stick War, the Creek War, or the Creek Rebellion, they went on the attack. It

Andrew Jackson led the Americans, Cherokee, Choctaw, and White Stick Creek in battle against the Red Stick Creek, effectively putting down the rebellion.

was because the warriors often wielded the red-painted "magic" war clubs Tecumseh had left them as a symbol of their strength that they were called the Red Sticks. The Red Sticks became extremely hostile not only to white settlers but to the pro-American Creek, or the White Sticks, as described in *Forked Tongues and Broken Treaties:*

> The hostiles . . . talked of war as they circulated the "magical" red war clubs from town to town accompanied by bundles of sticks indicating the number of days until a general attack. From town to town, as if by a pre-arranged signal, the war drums began their ominous cadence, and the Dance of the Lakes added wild rhythms to the scene of impending war. Hostiles began to kill livestock, fowls, and other "white" animals, while they also destroyed guns, ammunition, and farm implements gained in past treaties.[28]

Killing raids became common between Native Americans and white settlers, who pointed to the violence as further proof that the "savages" should be removed from the land.

On August 30, 1813, the temporary stockade at Fort Mims in Alabama was attacked by one thousand Red Sticks, resulting in the deaths of about four hundred settlers and soldiers. Angry Americans called for a reprisal against the Red Sticks, who retreated into the countryside under the leadership of two able tribesmen: Red Eagle, also known as William Weatherford, and Menewa. The American opposition was put in the hands of Andrew Jackson, an experienced officer, who gathered a force of thirty-five hundred soldiers allied with Cherokee, Choctaw, and White Stick Creek. For four months Jackson tracked the Red Sticks, but he was always one step behind them. Finally, he cornered them at a waterway junction called Horseshoe Bend in March 1814. After a whole day of battle, almost every Red Stick lay dead, ending the Creek rebellion. For the White Sticks it was a bittersweet victory, since they along with the Red Sticks were forced by treaty to give up more than half of their Alabama lands and part of Georgia as well. Menewa, one of the Red Stick leaders, echoed the fate of his people: "Last night I saw the sun set for the last time, and its light shine upon the treetops and the land and the water that I am never to look upon again."[29]

The Seminole Wars

Following the Red Stick War, Creek migration to Florida increased, swelling the Seminole population from two thousand to four thousand members. With the hostilities over, attention turned to the Seminole, who were known protectors of escaped slaves. Angry slaveholders called for government action, and Andrew Jackson, now a major general, was made responsible for solving the issue.

Pushmataha

Pushmataha was one of the greatest Choctaw chiefs of the early nineteenth century. He advocated peaceful relations with whites, believing that such civilities would protect Choctaw interests. He was fascinated by European culture, and not only adopted many white attributes but also encouraged other Native Americans to do so.

Pushmataha was born around 1764, but nothing is known of his parents. According to W. B. Morrison, in "The Story of Pushmataha, Historic Choctaw Chief," after he had grown into a warrior, he boasted that "Pushmataha has no ancestors; the sun was his father, the moon, his mother. A mighty storm swept the earth; midst the roar of thunder, the lightning split a mighty oak and Pushmataha stepped forth a full-fledged warrior."

Pushmataha was a gifted orator and dissuaded most Choctaw and Chickasaw warriors from uniting with Tecumseh when the Shawnee leader visited the tribes to persuade them to join his union of native peoples against the Americans. Pushmataha's reply to Tecumseh is quoted by Charlie Jones in "Memorial Exercises at the Grave of Pushmataha."

"If Tecumseh's words be true . . . then the Shawnees' experience with the whites has not been the same as that of the Choctaws. These white Americans buy our skins, our corn, our cotton . . . and other wares, and they give us fair ex-change [for] their cloth, their guns, their tools . . . and other things. . . . You all remember well the dreadful epidemic visited upon us last winter. During its darkest hours these neighbors whom we are now urged to attack responded generously to our needs. They doctored our sick; they clothed our suffering. . . . So in marked contrast with the experience of the Shawnees, it will be seen that the whites and Indians in this section are living on friendly and mutually beneficial terms."

Soon after Tecumseh departed, Pushmataha and several hundred warriors joined Andrew Jackson in pursuing the Red Stick Creek, whom he helped to defeat at the Battle of Horseshoe Bend. He became a brigadier general in the U.S. Army and fought alongside Jackson in the victorious battle against the British at New Orleans in 1814.

Pushmataha frequently went to Washington, D.C., to negotiate business for the Choctaw. During one such trip, he came down with pneumonia, and died December 24, 1824. He was buried in the Washington Congressional Cemetery. W. B. Morrison sums up Pushmataha's character in "The Story of Pushmataha," saying he was "a man with intuitive conception of honor and morals; a great general, brave . . . wise in council; a sane law-giver; a safe . . . leader; loyal in friendship and possessing a notable rugged honesty."

In 1814 he gathered a large military force and marched illegally into Florida, which was still Spanish territory. The four years he plunged through the wetlands burning Seminole towns and recapturing former slaves became known as the First Seminole War. After the military withdrew in 1818, Florida was annexed to the United States, opening the region to settlement.

The Second Seminole War began in 1835 when a group of Seminole and former slaves ambushed and killed more than a hundred soldiers who were on their way to round up the Native Americans for removal to the west. With the U.S. military in pursuit, a skilled orator and warrior named Osceola led the Seminole into hiding. In 1835, as hostilities began, Osceola spoke of the Seminole spirit: "You have guns, and so have we. You have powder and lead, and so have we. You have men and so have we. Your men will fight and so will ours, till the last drop of the Seminole's blood has moistened the dust of his hunting ground."[30] Between 1836 and 1838, Osceola and his warriors successfully eluded the military through masterful guerrilla tactics with which their pursuers were unfamiliar. The continuous heavy losses inflicted by the Seminole led the military on a quest to end Osceola's control of the resistance. Under the ruse of a white flag, he was lured into being captured and was thrown into a federal prison. Osceola died there in 1838, proud and unvan-

quished to the end. Although the war continued without him, the formal Seminole resistance gradually died out, and the warriors retreated deep into the swamps.

Unfair Laws

While many Native Americans were at war with the United States, the Cherokee were instead subjected to legal injustices. During the 1820s the state of Georgia passed a series of laws that were blatantly discriminatory against the Cherokee, "forbidding their judicial officers to hold court or their council to meet except to ratify land cessions, forbidding them to mine their own gold, authorizing a survey of their land and its disposal by lottery to Georgians."[31] Neither could they own land or vote. They were beaten, robbed, and killed for not complying, and their homes and businesses were burned.

The Cherokee attempted to contest these laws, but in the case of *Cherokee Nation v. Georgia* (1831), the Supreme Court stated that it had no authority to intervene because the Cherokee were not a foreign state. However, in 1832 a missionary friend, Samuel Worcester, sued Georgia for illegally abolishing Native American land ownership. In *Worcester v. Georgia*, Chief Justice John Marshall ruled in favor of the Cherokee, but Andrew Jackson, now president, scoffed at the decision, stating "Marshall has made his decision—now let him enforce it."[32] This callous attitude angered many Cherokee, setting the stage for conflict within the tribe.

Chief William McIntosh

William McIntosh was a controversial Creek leader of the early ninteenth century. He was the son of a Scot from a prestigious Georgia family, and his mother was a Creek member of the Wind clan, with whom he was raised.

During the Creek War, McIntosh supported the pro-American faction of the tribe and fought against the Red Sticks at the Battle of Horseshoe Bend in 1814. He was then made a brigadier general in the U.S. Army.

Following the war, McIntosh settled down on a plantation on the Chattahoochee River where he owned seventy-two slaves. He also served the U.S. Army during the First Seminole War and became famous for capturing a fort housing three hundred escaped black slaves.

McIntosh gained the enmity of the Creek tribe by signing the Treaty of Indian Springs in February 1825, which ceded the remaining Creek territory in Georgia for four hundred thousand dollars. It is a great debate whether he signed the treaty for personal gain or because he thought it was the best option for his people. In accordance with a promise by the Red Sticks to execute any tribesman who gave away Creek land without consent, McIntosh was killed in April 1825. He was shot inside his house, but managed to shoot back at his attackers. When the house was set afire he ran from it and was shot down. Still he did not succumb, but tried to get up, and was promptly stabbed in the heart. His estate was ransacked and his family left destitute, ignored by the Americans and shunned by the Creek.

William McIntosh, a Creek chief who serves in the U.S. Army.

The Treaty of New Echota

Tribal division arose between two groups that had very different ideas about the best strategy for Cherokee survival. The overwhelming majority of people supported the Ross Faction, which was headed by Principal Chief John Ross, a well-educated tribesman who had supported Cherokee efforts to assimilate European ways. Ross considered the Cherokee Nation a sovereign body whose territorial boundaries must be respected by the U.S. government. The Ross Faction was anti-removal and echoed the words of Dragging Canoe, chief of the Cherokee in 1768:

Cherokee chief John Ross advocated resisting American demands to move to Indian Territory.

> We had hoped that the white man would not be willing to travel beyond the mountains. Now that hope is gone. . . . [They] have settled upon Tsalagi (Cherokee) land. They wish to have that usurpation sanctioned by treaty. When that is gained, the same encroaching spirit will lead them upon other land of the Tsalagi (Cherokees). . . . Finally, the whole country, which the Tsalagi (Cherokees) and their fathers have so long occupied, will be demanded, and the remnant . . . will be compelled to seek refuge in some distant wilderness. There they will be permitted to stay only a short while, until they again behold the advancing banners of the same greedy host. . . . [T]he extinction of the whole race will be proclaimed. Should we not therefore run all risks, and incur all consequences, rather than to submit to further loss of our country? . . . We will hold our land.[33]

A small group supported the opposing Ridge Faction, led by councilman John Ridge, a former friend and counselor of Ross. Like Ross, Ridge had been a leader in the assimilation process. However, Ridge believed that the best option was for the Cherokee to migrate peaceably to Indian Territory, where they could take up their livelihoods again unimpeded.

The U.S. government was aware of the two factions and met secretly with members of the Ridge Faction at the Cherokee capital, New Echota, in 1835. Despite lack of authority, Ridge and several supporters signed a treaty that relinquished the remaining Cherokee lands in return for territory and provisions in Indian Territory. Outraged, Chief Ross and more than fifteen thousand Cherokee signed a petition citing the illegality of the Treaty of New Echota. The petition was ignored while the U.S. Senate rati-

fied the treaty, giving Jackson legal justification for removal. Just four years later, Ridge and several other signers of the treaty were murdered for violating a Cherokee law that imposed the death sentence on any tribesman who sold land without the consent of the Cherokee people.

Treaties such as New Echota secured the fate of the Five Civilized Tribes of the Southeast. The darkest years of all lay just ahead along the path to Indian Territory. David Folsom, a Choctaw, bemoaned this fate in 1830: "We have just heard of the ratification of the Choctaw Treaty. Our doom is sealed. There is no other course for us but to turn our faces to our new homes toward the setting sun."[34]

Chapter 7

Removal and the Reservations

Beginning in the first Jackson administration, pursuant to federal policy expressed in the Indian Removal Act of 1830, all the southeastern tribes were forcibly removed west to Indian Territory, lands that had been set aside for native peoples by an act of Congress in 1834. Many Native Americans suffered unimaginable horrors on the journey, but they carried with them the strength to rebuild their lives in the new land. On the eve of their departure, Levi Colbert, a Chickasaw quoted in *Through Indian Eyes*, reflected on the effect of the impending migration: "We never had a thought of exchanging our land for any other . . . fearing the consequences may be similar to transplanting an old tree, which would wither and die away."[35]

The Removal Gets Under Way: Choctaw, Creek, Chickasaw, and Cherokee

The Choctaw were the first to go, being herded in large groups onto boats as early as 1830, where many suffered from over-crowding and unsanitary conditions. Others were led by incompetent guides over a rugged 550-mile route, poorly clothed for the cold of winter travel. In 1831 the French visitor Alexis de Tocqueville described the scene:

> The Indians had their families with them, and they brought in their train the wounded and the sick, with children newly born and old men upon the verge of death. They possessed neither tents nor wagons, but only their arms and some provisions. . . . [There was] no cry, no sob . . . all were silent. The calamities were of ancient date, and they knew them to be irremediable. . . . [They] have been ruined by a competition which they had not the means of sustaining. They were isolated in their own country.[36]

By the end of 1832, the forty thousand Choctaw had been removed from their homes, of whom six thousand died from

71

Disease

The tribes of the Southeast were repeatedly struck by disease epidemics that sometimes killed more than half the population at a single time. Between the sixteenth and eighteenth centuries there were at least five recorded outbreaks of smallpox, four of measles, and several of influenza. Thousands suffered also from syphilis, tuberculosis, cholera, and other illnesses. Native Americans were extremely susceptible to European diseases that were nonexistent in North America prior to the 1500s, and to which they had no natural immunity. The traditional cures had no effect on these deadly diseases. Some cures even worsened the effects—in the sweat lodge communicable disease spread even faster, and the custom of following the sweat lodge with a jump in a cold stream often proved to be such a shock to people's immune systems that they readily contracted pneumonia, which killed thousands.

Often the inability of medicine men to effect cures led to whole communities doubting their spiritual power. The sacred objects were tossed aside by demoralized healers. Thus the emotional base so critical for healing was greatly undermined. In addition, when whole communities fell ill at the same time, often no one would be left to hunt, tend the crops, or take care of the sick. As a result, winter could arrive with little or no provisions set aside.

The most common and devastating disease was smallpox. Aside from the huge numbers of people it killed, the survivors of smallpox bore a burden too cruel for many to live with, for they were left with severe permanent pockmark scars all over their bodies. To a people who greatly valued the strength and beauty of their own bodies, this created a shameful appearance. James Adair describes in *The History of the American Indians* how Native Americans typically dealt with this: "Some shot themselves, others cut their throats, some stabbed themselves with knives and others with sharp-pointed canes; many threw themselves with sullen madness into the fire and there slowly expired, as if they had been utterly divested of the native power of feeling pain."

cholera, dysentery, influenza, and pneumonia, as well as exposure to the cold.

The Creek migration began in the summer of 1836, with 2,500 people being crowded onto two small riverboats. After journeying down the Arkansas River to the Gulf of Mexico and then back up the Mississippi, they traveled overland to Indian Territory. Along the two-month trip over 1,000 died from dysentery and cholera, in addition to the 311 Creek who perished when their steamboat sank. By the end of 1837, 15,000 Creek had left the southeast.

Next to go were the Chickasaw, although no land had been set aside for them in Indian Territory. Most of them traveled by boat up the Arkansas River during 1837. The Chickasaw fared much better than the other tribes as their boats were sanitary and not a single outbreak of disease occurred, allowing most of them to survive the trip. When they arrived in the west, the Chickasaw, with nowhere else to turn, had to ask permission to live in the western part of Choctaw territory.

The Cherokee suffered the most. In May 1838 U.S. troops rounded up eight thousand men, women, and children and imprisoned them in stockades while their homes were ransacked and their belongings were stolen by hordes of settlers. James Mooney wrote, "families at dinner were startled by the sudden gleam of bayonets in the doorway and rose up to be driven with blows and oaths along the trail that led to the stockade. Men were seized in their fields . . . women were taken from their [spinning] wheels and children from their play."[37] Food and other provisions ran low in the stockades, where some Cherokee lived for months. Many succumbed to disease and malnutrition before the migration even began.

The Trail of Tears

Finally in October 1838 the Cherokee were released from the stockades and

Cherokee Indians travel the Trail of Tears to Indian Territory. One quarter of those who made this journey died from exposure and disease.

loaded into wagons to begin the overland journey. The trip lasted from three to five months in the bitter winter cold, during which a quarter of the Cherokee people perished from exposure, tuberculosis, pneumonia, and other diseases. Decades later, an army private, John G. Burnett, recalled the journey, which the Cherokee called *oosti ganuhnuh dunaclohiluh* or "the trail where they cried":

> One can never forget the sadness and solemnity of that morning. . . . When . . . the wagons started rolling many of the children rose to their feet and waved their little hands good-by to their mountain homes,

knowing they were leaving them forever. Many . . . did not have blankets and . . . had been driven from home barefooted. . . . On the morning of November the 17th we encountered a terrific sleet and snow storm with freezing temperatures and from that day until we reached the end . . . the sufferings of the Cherokees were awful. The trail of the exiles was a trail of death. They had to sleep in the wagons and on the ground without fire. And I have known as many as twenty-two of them to die in one night of pneumonia due to ill treatment, cold, and

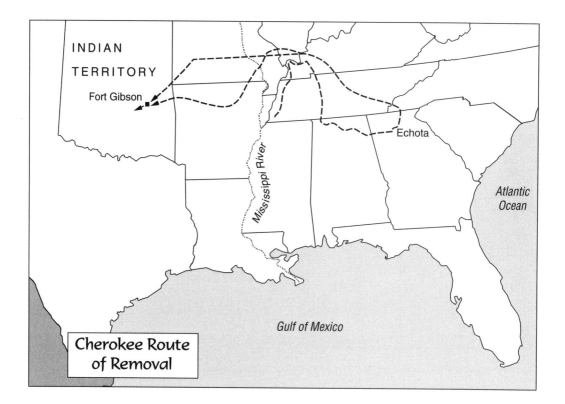

Cherokee Route of Removal

exposure. . . . The long painful journey . . . ended . . . with four-thousand silent graves reaching from the foothills of the Smoky Mountains to . . . Indian territory in the West. . . . Somebody must explain the streams of blood that flowed in the Indian country. . . . I wish I could forget it all, but the picture of 645 wagons lumbering over the frozen ground with their cargo of suffering humanity still lingers in my memory.[38]

Despite the suffering and even though the outlook remained bleak, Cherokee Stand Watie summed up the indomitable will of the Native American to survive:

I believe it is in the power of the Indians unassisted, but united and determined, to hold their country. We cannot expect to do this without serious losses and many privations, but we possess the spirit of our fathers and are resolved never to be enslaved by an inferior race, and trodden under the feet of an ignorant and insolent foe, we, the Creeks, Choctaws, Chickasaws, Seminoles, and Tsalagi (Cherokees), never can be conquered.[39]

The Seminole had been scheduled for removal in 1835, but Osceola's resistance delayed it for seven years. After the end of the Second Seminole War, nearly all the Seminole were hunted by military bloodhounds, captured, and shipped off to Indian Territory. Because the United States did not consider them a separate group, they were settled on Creek lands, resulting in years of conflict between the two peoples.

About three hundred Seminole fled deep into the Everglades and Big Cypress Swamp where they remained until after 1900. Many small groups of other tribes managed to elude the military and survive for decades hidden in the hills, woods, or swamps of their homelands. A few hundred Cherokee hid deep in caves in the Great Smokies, while Creek retreated to impenetrable regions of Alabama. A few Choctaw concealed themselves in less hospitable regions in Mississippi.

Rebuilding After Removal

During the years following the removal, the Five Civilized Tribes labored to rebuild their communities and society as they had been in the Southeast. Republican forms of government were established and new churches, farms, and businesses were opened. The first public school system was in place by 1841. Much of this was accomplished with the help of Christian missionaries. According to "Choctaw Nation History," "The Choctaws adjusted quickly to their new homeland. Missionaries were sent to Oklahoma Territory representing several denominations. . . . These missionaries established good rapport with the Choctaws, and early impressed upon the Choctaws the importance and need for a formal education if they were to co-exist with the white man."[40]

The Trail of Tears

This is a personal account of nine-year-old Samuel Cloud's experience of the Cherokee removal. His great-great-grandson, Michael Rutledge, records his story in his paper "Forgiveness in the Age of Forgetfulness."

"I am playing with my friends when white men in uniforms ride up to our home. . . . My mother and I are taken by several men to where their horses are and are held there at gun point. . . .From my mother I feel fear. I am filled with fear, too. What is going on? . . . My father is walking by the other men, talking in low, angry tones. . . . They lead us to a stockade. They herd us into this pen like we are cattle. No one was given time to gather any possessions. The nights are still cold . . . and we do not have enough blankets to go around. My mother holds me at night to keep me warm. That is the only time I feel safe. . . . My mother . . . take(s) me aside one day. 'Your father died last night,' [my mother tells me]. . . . I do not understand what this means. . . . It is now Fall. It seems like forever since I was clean. The stockade is nothing but mud. . . . The soldiers suddenly tell us we are to follow them. . . . We walk across the frozen earth. . . . The cold seeps through my clothes. I wish I had my blanket. . . . I remember my father's smile. It seems like so long ago. . . . Each day . . . they bury the dead in shallow graves. . . . As we walk past white towns, the whites come out to watch us pass. . . . I wish they would stop staring. I wish it were them walking in this misery and I were watching them. It is because of them that we are walking. . . . We are all cold and the snow and ice seem to hound us, claiming our people one by one. . . . My mother is coughing now. She looks worn. Her hands and face are burning hot. . . . I don't want to leave her alone. I just want to sit with her. I want her to stroke my hair. . . . When she feels me by her side, she opens her blanket and lets me in. . . . I can make it another day, I know, because she is here. . . . When I woke up she was cold. I tried to wake her up, but she lay there. The soft warmth she once was, she is no more. I kept touching her, as hot tears stream down my face. She couldn't leave me. She wouldn't leave me. . . . My aunt begins to wail. I will never forget that wail. . . . I am alone. I want to cry. I want to scream in rage. I can do nothing. We bury her in a shallow grave by the road. I will never forget that lonesome hill of stone that is her final bed, as it fades from my sight. . . . I hate those white soldiers who took us from our home (and) make us keep walking through the snow and ice toward this new home that none of us ever wanted. I hate the people who killed my father and mother. . . . None of those white people are here to say they are sorry that I am alone. None of them care about me or my people. All they ever saw was the color of our skin."

Largely through the efforts of early missionaries, the Choctaw accepted a religion and code of morals very different from the belief system of their ancestors, established an educational system foreign to traditional practices, adopted the constitution and legal system developed in another culture, and modified their agriculture and commerce to conform to a complex economy set up by others. In 1854 the Indian Appropriations Act was passed, which gave Congress the authority to establish Indian reservations and recognized the tribes as separate nations under the protection of the federal government, although the United States still considered the Seminole as part of the Creek tribe and the Chickasaw as part of the Choctaw tribe.

Traditional enmities had to be set aside in order to thrive as neighbors within Indian Territory. Choctaw and Chickasaw tolerated each other peacefully. The Red Sticks and White Sticks reunited as Creek, who also strived to resolve their differences with the Seminole. In 1856 the Seminole finally gained recognition as a nation in its own right and was granted its own territory. That same year the Chickasaw moved off Choctaw land onto their own territory to the west.

The unity of the Five Tribes was essential to provide a force against angry Plains Indians, who regarded them as unwelcome encroachers upon their lands. Despite this conflict, as well as bigotry from nearby Americans, many members of the Five Tribes were successful in politics and business within the reservations. For decades they prospered, unencumbered by outsiders. However, as the twentieth century drew near, all they had worked for was once again threatened by the greed of white settlers.

Land Allotment and the Dawes Commission

In 1866 the Five Tribes, who up to this time were the sole and original occupants of Indian Territory, signed new treaties with the United States that penalized them for their support of the Confederacy during the Civil War. These treaties required the Five Tribes to relinquish part of Indian Territory to serve as reservations for other displaced tribes such as the Apache, Kiowa, and Cheyenne, who had twenty years before battled with the Five Tribes over their western homelands that were now appropriated and administered by whites.

Then in 1887, with the passage of the Dawes General Allotment Act, tribal governments were terminated and reservation lands were divided into quarter sections, which were parcels of land equaling 160 acres. Each head of a family was to receive one-quarter of a section, with unmarried adults, orphans, and children under the age of eighteen years getting smaller amounts of land. Land remaining after all qualified tribesmen had received their parcels was to be sold to settlers. Though vast by today's urban standards, the allotments were far from generous, for much of the land was useless for farming or hunting.

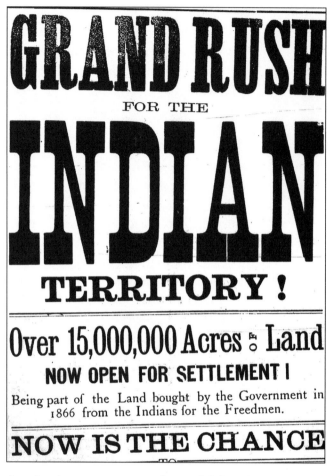

GRAND RUSH

FOR THE

INDIAN

TERRITORY !

Over 15,000,000 Acres of Land

NOW OPEN FOR SETTLEMENT !

Being part of the Land bought by the Government in 1866 from the Indians for the Freedmen.

NOW IS THE CHANCE

An advertisement announces the availability of land in Indian Territory for white settlement.

At first the territory of the Five Tribes was excluded from allotment by a special provision of the Dawes Act. But as more and more whites arrived in Indian Territory, they pressured the U.S. government to open the regions surrounding the Five Tribes' reservations to settlement. In response, an unassigned region called Oklahoma Territory was opened for settlement in 1889. Because the newly designated U.S. territory did not include any actual reservation land, and because the Five Tribes did not view the Dawes Act as a threat, many members accepted the change without protest. As the surrounding lands filled up, whites clamored to open up some of the reservation lands.

Assuming their lands to be protected from white encroachment by the Dawes Act proved to be a grave mistake for the Five Tribes. Only ten years later Congress passed a law extending the jurisdiction of the Dawes Act to the territory of the Five Tribes. Immediately a body that became known as the Dawes Commission was created solely for the purpose of setting up a schedule for dissolving the tribal governments and allotting the reservation lands of the Five Tribes. An Oklahoma Creek commented on the commission, saying, "Egypt had its locusts, Asiatic countries their cholera, England its black plague. But it was left for unfortunate Indian Territory to be afflicted with the worst scourge of the 19th Century, the Dawes Commission."[41] Once again they stood at a crossroads, faced with the option of living on allotted land or leaving their homes.

Oklahoma Statehood

By 1905 the tribal territories were gone, with almost 4 million acres sold and 15.8 million acres allotted as parcels. In 1907 Indian Territory was merged with Oklahoma Territory and became the state of Oklahoma. In this new state, which had once been the sole property of the Five Tribes, only 5.3 percent of the population was Native American.

Although scattered about without any cohesive political body, many Native American communities managed to survive. But without control over their own territory, government, and livelihoods, their former prosperity succumbed to competition from white businesses, which greatly outnumbered those of Native Americans. Faced with bigotry and

---

People of the Southeast in the American Civil War

When the Civil War erupted, the Five Civilized Tribes were divided over loyalty to the Union, joining the Confederacy, or remaining neutral. Situated in Oklahoma, they were much closer to the South, and with their annuities cut off from the federal government, most tribesmen threw their support to the Confederacy.

The Creek formed a Confederate regiment, as did the Seminole. The Choctaw and the Chickasaw together organized three regiments that fought for the South, and saw especially heavy battle at the end of the war. The Cherokee formed two Confederate regiments, one of which was led by Stand Watie, a relative of John Ridge. Watie was commissioned a brigadier general, and was the last Confederate general to surrender at the end of the war.

A third of the Seminole in Oklahoma migrated to Kansas to support the Union.

Many from other tribes in Indian Territory also went to Kansas and formed the First Regiment of Indian Home Guards. A number of Seminole blacks, former slaves who had escaped to Florida and joined the Seminole before the removal, served with the First Colored Infantry and participated in taking the Confederate army supply depot in 1863 in Honey Springs, Indian Territory (now Oklahoma).

With the defeat of the South in 1865, the Five Civilized Tribes were punished for having supported the Confederacy. Not only were they forced by treaty to cede lands in Indian Territory for settlement by other displaced tribes, but they had to allow two railroads to be built through their lands. They were also obligated to adopt freed blacks into their tribes and to give them full property rights.

Seminole Patchwork

During the twentieth century, Seminole women developed their popular patchwork technique that involves stitching strips of fabric together, cutting, and stitching again to create many different designs.

In the late 1800s the Seminole began to acquire hand-operated sewing machines, which, over time, transformed the way they made garments. The first designs were bars of alternating colors or a sawtooth pattern. By 1920 many new designs had been created, and Seminole clothing became more and more intricate.

The patchwork process is described by Colin F. Taylor and William C. Sturtevant in *The Native Americans: The Indigenous People of North America:*

"In patchwork, patterned cloth is first torn into long strips which are then sewn together to produce a band of striped cloth. The band is then snipped into several pieces which are arranged side by side or offset and sewn together into a long band. This technique allows for an astonishing variety of designs, and a woman usually uses several bands of varying designs in making one garment. The bands are then sewn together to form a whole piece of cloth that can be cut into patterns and sewn. The final product is a very colorful patchwork garment with a variety of intricate, detailed designs."

The traditional garments made from patchwork are women's skirts and blouses, and men's "belted" jackets. Today the patchwork is a cultural symbol for the Seminole and a popular tourist's item at craft and art shops.

Seminole patchwork, developed in the early twentieth century, is still popular today.

legal and political oppression, an age of poverty and hopelessness settled over the Five Civilized Tribes as they moved forward into the twentieth century. Carl Whitman, a Hidatsa tribal chairman, echoed this statement:

> We should really be used to these broken promises, but it seems like each one never loses its punch. . . . Sociologists have concluded that when you impose a change on any group of people there are three consequences. One is hostility, one is apathy, and the other is self-destruction. These are good theories. They have all come to pass. I have witnessed these.[42]

Chapter 8

People of the Southeast Today

Despite the loss of much of their culture and the hardship endured in centuries past, Native Americans are today striving to reclaim their heritage and assert their rights. For most of the twentieth century they have been treated like second-class citizens, incapable of caring for themselves. The people of the Southeast are constantly challenged by the need to function in two very different cultures; as a result, many have lost tribal identity, a sense of heritage, and their ancestral language. In 1906 the noted ethnologist John R. Swanton observed that the old traditions of the people of the Southeast were "now so completely discarded [that] practically all the younger people know nothing about it, and even the older ones can furnish only fragmentary information on the subject."[43]

In 1890 the total Native American population had dwindled to a mere 248,000, and it was assumed they were on the brink of becoming an extinct race. However, by 1990 the population had swelled to 2.75 million, and today survival seems guaranteed. Yet since the turn of the twentieth century, Native Americans have faced everything from brutal massacres to alcoholism, depression, and high unemployment. A general despondency combined with a lack of education left many tribes unable to generate the money needed for adequate health care, schools, or businesses able to compete in today's fast-paced market.

Survival in the Twentieth Century

During the first half of the twentieth century, many Native Americans of the Southeast lived without educational or job opportunities. Many of them lived in poverty and suffered from ill health. The statistics from the 1960s are staggering: diabetes was four times as common compared to the general population; infant mortality was three-and-a-half times and teen suicide was ten times the national average; the life expectancy for a Native

American was forty-four years, compared to seventy-one years for white Americans.

These health problems, as well as criminal activity, were largely attributed to the high rate of alcoholism among Native Americans. The alcoholism, in turn, was believed to be due to historical, social, and cultural factors. Many drank to alleviate depression resulting from poverty, bigotry, and a loss of cultural identity, deepened by the lack of autonomy created by government assistance programs. A picture of life for the Choctaw around 1914 is described in *Indians of the Southeast*:

In Mississippi . . . groups of Choctaws, a few hundred each, lived in squalor on abandoned, worn-out lands. Some of the women wove traditional cane baskets to barter with local white housewives for food for their children. . . . The Choctaws, discouraged from attending Mississippi public schools, had no schools of their own. Housing was makeshift for these poorly fed and poorly clothed Indians who were subject to unending racial prejudice and were stereotyped as "dumb, lazy, and slow."[44]

Native American Suffrage

During World War I a significant number of Native Americans joined the armed forces of the United States. At the end of the war nearly seventeen thousand Native Americans had served.

Native Americans joined the medical corps, the engineering corps, the cavalry, and all other military branches. They were allowed to defer the draft, however, because they were not citizens, but 30 percent of the male population, twice the average for the nation, served.

After returning from the war, many Native American veterans were discontented with their noncitizen status. The words of Charles Eastman, a Santee Sioux, echoed this sentiment in *Through*

Indian Eyes: "All we ask is full citizenship. Why not? We offered our services and our money in this war, and more in proportion to our number and means than any other race or class of the population." In 1919 the U.S. government recognized the contribution of Native Americans to the war effort and granted citizenship to those who were honorably discharged.

Just a few years later Senator Charles Curtis, a Kansa and Osage Indian, proposed legislation that granted citizenship to all Native Americans and protected their property rights. Full citizenship was finally extended to all native peoples in 1924 with the passage of this bill.

The Wheeler-Howard Act of 1934 was intended to eradicate many of these social problems by providing Native Americans with paternalistic government programs and subsidies. This law restored existing surplus lands to Native American tribes and gave them the right to organize tribal governments. Native American individuals had the option of voluntarily transferring allotments to tribal ownership. According to the Wheeler-Howard Act, substantial government loans were available to Native American businesses or for students at vocational or trade schools. Unfortunately, such programs did more harm than good because they fostered the impression that Native Americans were not capable of taking care of themselves. Paternalism failed because it did not motivate people to solve their problems, nor did it train them how to do it.

The response to this failure was a policy called "termination," in reality several laws and actions passed by Congress in the 1950s, which once again terminated the tribal governments of all Native American tribes as well as the Wheeler-Howard programs and subsidies. Termination laws provided incentives to persuade people to migrate from the reservations to urban areas, where they might be blended into the general population. Unfortunately, many of the promised incentives, such as job opportunities, were never realized. Earl Old Person, a Blackfoot tribal chairman, commented on the pressure to migrate to the cities, saying, "Why is it so important that Indians be brought into the 'mainstream of

American life?' I would not know how to interpret the phrase to my people. The closest I would be able to come would be 'a big, wide river.' Am I then to tell my people that they will be thrown into the Big Wide River of the United States?"[45]

Termination forced hundreds of youths to move to the city for better opportunities, due to the closure of reservation businesses. However, they were unprepared for the fast pace of urban life and lacked the skills needed for many jobs. Many returned to the reservations disillusioned, but with a new awareness of themselves as an ethnic group—an awareness that had been growing in Native American schoolchildren for several decades already.

Pan-Indianism and Red Power

Throughout the twentieth century children left the Oklahoma reservations to attain an education at distant boarding schools. The experience was mainly detrimental in that the curriculum was usually biased in favor of the European perspective and was taught in English, harboring low respect both for the students as individuals and for their heritage. There was, however, one very positive and unexpected side effect. Since many students came from different tribes, as they got to know each other they began to understand that the plight of their own people was the common plight of others. Students banded together in an effort to unite all Native Americans as a single ethnic group.

The groups of youths who had lived in cities also began to unite, and through the

Native Americans march in Washington D.C., protesting what they perceive as anti-Indian legislation in Congress.

1970s and 1980s a cultural movement called Pan-Indianism evolved. This movement called for Native Americans to rise above tribal differences to tackle common problems, and to celebrate and promote their various heritages.

Shared concerns with other dispossessed groups such as African Americans led to the more politically active Red Power movement of the 1970s, which focused on the enforcement and recognition of all legislation enacted on the behalf of Native Americans since colonial times. The "Declaration of Indian Purpose," written in 1961, summarized the reasons behind the Red Power movement:

> When our lands are taken . . . scattering our people and threatening our . . . existence, it grieves us to be told that

a money payment is the equivalent of all things we surrender. . . . Were we paid a thousand times the market value of our lost holdings, still the payment would not suffice. Money never mothered the Indian people as the land has mothered them, nor have any people become more closely attached to the land, religiously and traditionally. . . . This is not special pleading. We ask only that the United States be true to its own traditions and set an example to the world in fair dealing.

When Indians speak of the continent they yielded, they are not referring only to the loss of some millions of acres in real estate. They have in mind that the land supported a universe of things they knew, valued, and loved.

. . . [T]hey mean to hold the scraps and parcels as earnestly as any small nation or ethnic group was ever determined to hold to identity and survival.[46]

Protests and media publicity were the major tactics used by Red Power activists, although some militant property seizures were utilized in a few instances to force government officials to listen to their grievances and honor their claims.

In the 1970s the various termination laws were repealed and Native Americans were allowed once more to organize under their respective tribal identities and establish tribal governments. The Indian Self-Determination and Educational Assistance Act of 1975 created a compromise between termination and paternalism in that it allowed tribes to contract with federal departments for various educational, health care, or other programs. This system allows individual tribes to determine what their needs are and to make decisions about whether to use federal assistance to meet them. Along with taking responsibility for preserving their culture and their rights, the native people of the Southeast are working toward self-sufficiency by establishing various business enterprises.

The Choctaw and the Chickasaw Today

The great majority of Choctaw are members of the Choctaw Nation of Oklahoma, located in the southeastern portion of the state. About a thousand reside in the homelands in Mississippi. The Choctaw people run the Choctaw Plaza and Smoke Shop, which averages $1.5 million in monthly gross sales in addition to the two other smoke shops in operation. Revenue and jobs are also created with a shopping center, the Arrowhead Resort Hotel and Gaming Center, three bingo halls, and the Choctaw Nation Finishing Company.

The Chickasaw, who inhabit south central Oklahoma, are also implementing economic strategies designed to form job opportunities and bring in revenue for local schools and social programs. The Chickasaw have been very proactive in mingling with the nonreservation public, and in 1997 their businesses increased by

Wilma Mankiller

Wilma Mankiller was the first female principal chief of the Cherokee Nation of Oklahoma. She overcame great personal tragedy to keep a lifelong commitment to serving her people.

Mankiller was born in Tahlequah, Oklahoma, in November 1945 to a Cherokee father and a Dutch-Irish mother. Her family lived a very poor existence until she was ten years old, when her father decided to move them to California on the promise of government assistance and employment. However, after they arrived in San Francisco, the money and jobs were not forthcoming.

After completing high school, Mankiller attended San Francisco State University, where she met and married Hugo Olaya de Bardi. The couple had two daughters, one in 1964 and one in 1966. It was during her college years that she also met members of the All Tribes group, which later seized Alcatraz Island and reclaimed it for Native Americans. Following this event, Mankiller realized that her life mission was to work for the interests of the Cherokee.

As she became increasingly involved with activism, her marriage suffered, a fact detailed in a quote from Mankiller's autobiography from the Gale Group Women's History website: "Once I began to become more independent, more active with school and in the community, it became difficult to keep my marriage together. Before that, Hugo had viewed me as someone he had rescued from a very bad life." After she and Hugo were divorced in 1974, she continued to volunteer her services to Native American causes.

In 1976 Mankiller returned to Oklahoma. She attended the University of Arkansas as a graduate student, driving about ninety miles daily between her home near Tahlequah and the university in Fayetteville. One morning as she was driving home from classes she was seriously injured in a car accident. Soon afterwards, she discovered she was suffering from a muscle disease called myasthenia gravis. In addition, she developed kidney disease, for which she received a transplant in 1990. In spite of these tragedies she continued to work for her people.

Wilma Mankiller served as principal chief of the Cherokee Nation of Oklahoma between 1985 and 1995; she was inducted into the National Women's Hall of Fame in 1994. Although she continued to be plagued by illness, including hospitalization for cancer in 1996, Mankiller remained active in community projects for the Cherokee and frequently lectured on Native American issues.

12 percent. The Chickasaw Nation owns and operates the KADA radio station, Smoke Signals Computer Company, the Chickasaw Lodge and Restaurant, and various gaming centers, tobacco shops, and travel plazas.

The Creek and the Seminole Today

The Muskogee Creek Nation is based in Oklahoma and in northern Georgia. The Oklahoma population of forty-four thousand is supported by tribal enterprises such as travel plazas and extensive agricultural developments.

The Seminole are represented by two groups, one in Oklahoma and the other in Florida, both of which maintain the traditional division into matrilineal clans. The Seminole Nation of Oklahoma has seen a revival of the ancient religion, which revolves around the Stomp Dance, a derivation of the Busk (Green Corn) Dance. Although the nation is located in some of the most economically depressed counties of the state, the Seminole are striving to increase job and business opportunities among their members.

The two thousand members of the Seminole tribe of Florida are descendants of the three hundred who escaped the removal in the nineteenth century. The population is spread between six reservations in the state of Florida. Although most Seminole are

Saving the Florida Wetlands

The Seminole tribe of Florida is actively campaigning for the protection of the Everglades. This endeavor is very important to a people whose heritage depends on the ecosystem and the land. The tribe recognized the threat of man to the region and set up several projects designed to preserve the land and natural water systems.

One project involves implementing the Clean Water Act on behalf of the Environmental Protection Agency (EPA). The Seminole adopted water quality standards for the Florida reservations and installed a state-of-the-art monitoring system.

Other projects include spill prevention plans for storage tanks and removal plans for underground tanks. The Everglades Restoration Initiative is an ongoing project that will impact the quality and quantity of water flow off the Big Cypress Reservation into the Everglades. It will measure the effect of development on the region and will increase water storage capacity. Besides the benefits to the natural environment, the system will also store irrigation water and improve flood control.

Christian, many continue to respect and consult traditional medicine men. Funds for schools and other public systems come mainly from profits from gaming and tourism. Citrus groves and cattle also generate substantial revenue. In addition, the tribe publishes a newspaper, the *Seminole Tribune*, and operates the Seminole Broadcasting Department, which has three sister stations.

The Cherokee Today

The Cherokee are the largest Native American group today, with 308,000 members nationwide. Like the rest of the original people of the Southeast, they have established many business enterprises, including two gaming facilities and Cherokee Nation Industries, Inc., a multimillion dollar supplier to several major defense contractors. The Eastern Band of Cherokee is located in western North Carolina on the Qualla Boundary Reservation. Established in the nineteenth century, qualla is the domain of the descendants of the few hundred Cherokee who escaped into the mountains to avoid forced removal in 1838. The major sources of revenue for the Eastern Band are gaming halls and tourism.

Like many other Native American peoples, the Cherokee have come under fire

A member of the Cherokee Nation, the largest group of Native Americans in the United States.

for their high-stakes gambling enterprises. But there is no denying the ability of these gaming halls to reap enough money for many Native Americans to stay off government subsidies. As Donald L. Fixico,

Will Rogers

Will Rogers was best known as a folksy humorist who told the simple truth in common words. He was also a Hollywood star, a humanitarian, and cowboy.

Rogers was born in 1879 to Cherokee parents living on a ranch in Indian Territory. He was one of eight siblings, four of whom did not survive to adulthood. He grew up learning how to lasso and dropped out of school in the tenth grade to become a cowboy. He was so good at lassoing that he made it into the *Guinness Book of World Records*.

His lasso talent got him jobs performing in wild west shows and vaudeville, where he first tried humor. His jokes reflected a deeper philosophy, paramount of which was his fondness for mankind. According to the official Will Rogers website, "I never met a man I didn't like" was his motto. As his fame grew, he starred in Broadway shows and did a total of seventy-one Hollywood films in the 1920s and 1930s. He also worked as a radio broadcaster and wrote syndicated newspaper columns. He never stopped observing, reading, and learning, and he wrote six books over his lifetime.

Rogers's opinion was highly valued, and he was often a guest at the White House. He earned friendships with presidents, senators, and even foreign kings. He traveled often and learned as much as he could about people all over the world. He generously contributed his own money to disaster victims and organizations such as the Red Cross and Salvation Army.

Despite his fame and fortune, Rogers remained a Cherokee and a cowboy at heart. A quote from the Cherokees of California website describes his response to being asked if he was an American citizen. He replied with characteristic dry humor, "Well, I think I am. My folks were Indian. Both my mother and father had Cherokee blood in them. . . . 'Course we're not the Americans whose ancestors came over on the Mayflower, but we met them at the boat when they landed." His favorite moments were spent at home with his wife, Betty, and their four children on their ranches in Oklahoma and California. He preferred to spend his time horseback riding, roping steers, or playing polo.

Rogers also loved flying, and during a flight to Alaska in 1935 his plane crashed. He and the pilot, Wiley Post, both perished in the accident. The world mourned his death, and he became a great American legend. His eldest son, Will Rogers Jr., played his father in two of the many movies that commemorated his life and deeds.

who is part Creek and part Seminole, says, "We'd better call it Big Bingo these days because it's just not little bingo. It's in the thousands and millions of dollars."[47] Unfortunately not every tribe can reap the benefits of gaming, since many reservations are too far removed from populated areas to support such a huge enterprise. It is, however, an option that achieves financial security for many of the peoples of the Southeast.

Hope in the Twenty-First Century

At the begining of the twenty-first century, the Native American population is on the upswing and becoming increasingly aware of its heritage. In addition to successful business enterprises, such as the controversial gaming halls, Native Americans are reclaiming their independence through a revival in traditional arts. Today Catawba pottery and Cherokee baskets are much-coveted items for collectors of Native American art. Ancient crafts are part of the new curriculum of reservation schools,

Costumed dancers at a powwow celebrate native culture, unity, and shared traditions.

which embraces American history from the Native American perspective. Teaching is increasingly being done in native languages.

Pan-Indianism continues to promote a unified Native American heritage, widely celebrated during modern powwows. The powwow has become a symbol of renewal because it brings together many native cultures to celebrate shared traditions. Hazel Blake, a member of the Hidatsa, a Plains tribe, speaks for many Native Americans in her reasons for participating in these events: "If you come to these celebrations, you'll see all our young boys and girls with their feathers on. They are proud . . . proud to be Indians . . . proud to be wearing the eagle feather. And to us, that is very sacred."[48] Powwows involve speeches, traditional foods and arts, various dance exhibitions, and above all the reaffirmation of the spirit of Native American unity.

The original tribes of the Southeast can look to the future with hope for regaining their cultural identity and self-sufficiency as unique peoples. The promise of the twenty-first century will be secured by honoring the past, as Gary White Deer, a Chickasaw, said in 1994:

I think the Spirit, is the one thing we have to rely on. It has been handed to us as a live and precious coal. And each generation has to make that decision whether they want to blow on that coal to keep it alive or throw it away. . . . Our language, our histories and culture are like a big ceremonial fire that's been kicked and stomped and scattered. . . . Out in the darkness we can see those coals glowing. But our generation . . . Choctaw, Cherokee, Chickasaw, Creek, and Seminole—are coal gatherers. We bring the coals back, assemble them and breathe on them again, so we can spark a flame around which we might warm ourselves.[49]

Notes

Introduction: Evolution of a People

1. Quoted in Cherokees of California, "Words of Wisdom," 1999. www.power source.com/cocinc/articles/wisdom. htm.
2. Quoted in Editors of Reader's Digest, *Through Indian Eyes*. Pleasantville, NY: Reader's Digest, 1995, p. 378.

Chapter 1: Native Peoples of the Southeast

3. Creek Nation, "Muskoke Customs and Traditions," 1999, pp. 1–4. www.ocevnet. org/creek/customs.html.
4. Samuel Carter III, *Cherokee Sunset: A Nation Betrayed*. Garden City, NY: Doubleday, 1976, p. 18.
5. Quoted in Carter, *Cherokee Sunset*, p. 17.

Chapter 2: Villages and Clans of the Southeast Peoples

6. Creek Nation, "Muskoke Customs and Traditions," pp. 1–4.
7. Michael Rutledge, "Forgiveness in the Age of Forgetfulness," 1995. http://pages. tca.net/martikw/law.html.
8. Quoted in Jesse Burt and Robert B. Ferguson, *Indians of the Southeast: Then and Now*. New York: Abingdon Press, 1973, p. 109.

Chapter 3: Daily Life Among the People of the Southeast

9. Quoted in Editors of Reader's Digest, *Through Indian Eyes*, p. 37.
10. Quoted in Burt and Ferguson, *Indians of the Southeast*, p. 64.
11. Quoted in Burt and Ferguson, *Indians of the Southeast*, p. 75.
12. Quoted in Burt and Ferguson, *Indians of the Southeast*, p. 77.

Chapter 4: Keeping the Balance

13. Quoted in Virgil J. Vogel, *American Indian Medicine*. Norman: University of Oklahoma Press, 1970, p. 28.
14. Quoted in Susan H. DePrim, "The Legal History of the Choctaw Nation, Before Removal," *Bishinik*, February 1996, pp. 1–3. www.isd.net/mboucher/ choctaw/claw2.htm.
15. DePrim, "The Legal History of the Choctaw Nation, Before Removal," pp. 1–3.
16. Quoted in Vogel, *American Indian Medicine*, p. 26.
17. Burt and Ferguson, *Indians of the Southeast*, p. 65.
18. Quoted in Vogel, *American Indian Medicine*, pp. 100–101.
19. Quoted in Vogel, *American Indian Medicine*, p. 255.

20. Quoted in Vogel, *American Indian Medicine*, p. 53.

21. Len Green, "Choctaw Funeral Customs Were Changing Through the Years," *Bishinik*, July 1979, pp. 10–11. www.isd. net/mboucher/choctaw/burial1.htm.

Chapter 5: European Contact and Cultural Decline

22. Quoted in Editors of Reader's Digest, *Through Indian Eyes*, p. 46.

23. Quoted in Editors of Reader's Digest, *Through Indian Eyes*, p. 50.

24. Quoted in Editors of Reader's Digest, *Through Indian Eyes*, p. 51.

25. Editors of Reader's Digest, *Through Indian Eyes*, p. 63.

26. Quoted in Burt and Ferguson, *Indians of the Southeast*, p. 116.

27. Quoted in Ken Martin, "History of the Cherokee—1700 Through the Revolutionary War," 1996. http://pages. tca.net/martikw/1700thro.html.

Chapter 6: Dispossession: Difficult Years

28. Donald E. Worcester, ed., *Forked Tongues and Broken Treaties*. Caldwell, ID: Western Writers of America, 1975, p. 101.

29. Quoted in Editors of Reader's Digest, *Through Indian Eyes*, p. 66.

30. Quoted in Editors of Reader's Digest, *Through Indian Eyes*, p. 73.

31. Quoted in Worcester, *Forked Tongues and Broken Treaties*, p. 56.

32. Quoted in Editors of Reader's Digest, *Through Indian Eyes*, p. 71.

33. Quoted in Indigenous Peoples' Literature, "Tsalagi (Cherokee) Literature," 1999, p. 1. www.indians.org/welker/cherokee. htm.

34. Quoted in Editors of Reader's Digest, *Through Indian Eyes*, p. 72.

Chapter 7: Removal and the Reservations

35. Quoted in Editors of Reader's Digest, *Through Indian Eyes*, p. 67.

36. Quoted in Editors of National Geographic Society, *The World of the American Indian*. Washington, DC: National Geographic Society, 1974, p. 311.

37. Quoted in Worcester, *Forked Tongues and Broken Treaties*, p. 67.

38. The Cherokee Cultural Society of Houston, "John G. Burnett's Story of the Removal of the Cherokees," *Cherokee Messenger*, 1996, pp. 1–3. www.powersource.com/cherokee/ burnett.html.

39. Indigenous Peoples' Literature, "Tsalagi (Cherokee) Literature," p. 2.

40. Choctaw Nation, "Choctaw Nation History," 1999. www.choctawnation. com/history/choctaw_nation_ history. htm.

41. Quoted in Editors of Reader's Digest, *Through Indian Eyes*, p. 347.

42. Quoted in Editors of Reader's Digest, *Through Indian Eyes*, p. 374.

Chapter 8: People of the Southeast Today

43. Quoted in Burt and Ferguson, *Indians of the Southeast*, p. 230.

44. Burt and Ferguson, *Indians of the Southeast*, pp. 231–36.

45. Quoted in Editors of Reader's Digest, *Through Indian Eyes*, p. 363.

46. Quoted in Burt and Ferguson, *Indians of the Southeast*, pp. 239–40.

47. Quoted in Editors of Reader's Digest, *Through Indian Eyes*, p. 375.

48. Quoted in Editors of Reader's Digest, *Through Indian Eyes*, p. 378.

49. Quoted in Cherokees of California, "Words of Wisdom."

For Further Reading

Books

Cottie Burland, *North American Indian Mythology*. Rev. ed. New York: Peter Bedrick Books, 1985. This book describes the myths, spirits, and spiritual customs of many tribes across North America, including those of the Southeast.

Nicole Claro, *The Cherokee Indians*. New York: Chelsea House, 1992. Part of the Junior Library of American Indians series, this book examines the history, culture, and future of the Cherokee tribe.

Editors of Time-Life Books, *Tribes of the Southern Woodlands*. Alexandria, VA: Time-Life Books, 1994. Part of a Time-Life series, this book beautifully illustrates and describes the culture and history of the people of the Southeast.

Grant Foreman, *The Five Civilized Tribes*. Norman: University of Oklahoma Press, 1934. Although somewhat dated, this book provides a detailed look at the heritage and history of the Seminole, Creek, Chickasaw, Choctaw, and Cherokee tribes.

Shirley Glubok, *The Art of the Southeastern Indians*. New York: Macmillan, 1978. Full of photographs and elaborate illustrations, this books covers a wide range of art forms of the people of the Southeast, including weaponry, clothing, basketry, and pottery.

Michael D. Green, *The Creeks*. New York: Chelsea House, 1990. Part of the Junior Library of American Indians series, this book describes the history, culture, and future prospects of the Creek tribe.

Arlene B. Hirschfelder and Beverly R. Singer, eds., *Rising Voices: Writings of Young Native Americans*. San Ramon, CA: Ivy

Books, 1993. This inspiring collection of poems and essays written by Native American youths during the last one hundred years reflects the history, tragedy, and hope of various North American tribes.

Philip Koslow and B. Marvis, *The Seminole Indians*. New York: Chelsea House, 1994. Another book from the Junior Library of American Indians series, it examines the history, culture, and future of the Seminole tribe.

Joanne F. Oppenheim, *Osceola: Seminole Warrior*. Mahwah, NJ: Troll Communications, 1979. This book chronicles the life and achievements of one of the most celebrated members of the Seminole tribe.

Melissa Schwartz, *Wilma Mankiller: Principal Chief of the Cherokees*. New York: Chelsea House, 1994. This book is part of the North American Indians of Achievement Series and details both the sadness and hope of Mankiller's youth, her years of self-discovery in college, her commitment to improving the lives of the Cherokee people, and the tragedies she has overcome during her adult life. There is also an excellent introduction to the history of the Cherokee tribe.

Sylvia Whitman, *Hernando De Soto and the Explorers of the American South*. Boston: Horn Book, 1991. This objective account details the Spanish exploration of 1539–1543, including the treatment of Native Americans and the often tragic results. Includes good maps and excellent illustrations.

Bill Yenne, *The Encyclopedia of North American Indian Tribes*. 1986. Reprint. Avenel, NJ: Crescent Books, 1995. This book includes beautiful illustrations and a short profile of nearly every Native American tribe known to North America, no matter how small. Language, type of housing and subsistence, and some history are highlighted in each entry.

Websites

Cherokees of California (www.powersource.com/cocinc/articles/wisdom.htm). This site contains links to information on

Cherokee history and customs, including recipes, hymns, myths, the seven sacred colors, and even offers Cherokee language lessons.

Chickasaw Nation (www.chickasaw.com). This is the official home page of one of the Five Civilized Tribes, and includes information on current government and community issues, businesses, and the culture and heritage of the Chickasaw people.

Choctaw Nation (www.choctawnation.com). This site offers information on current events and business enterprises, as well as articles on clothing, the Trail of Tears, tribal history, and customs. The site also provides links to Choctaw stories and legends.

Creek Nation (www.ocevnet.org/creek/customs.html). This site contains brief information on agriculture, clans, clothing, history, ceremonies, and towns of the Creek, as well as interesting details about the concept of time, the sacred number of four, and the inspiration of nature in the lives of the Creek.

Official Homepage of the Seminole Nation of Oklahoma (www.cowboy.net/native/seminole). This site provides information on the politics, education, religion, geographical location, population, and history of the tribe, which originated from the Creek. It also offers a huge number of links to other tribal home pages, Native American organizations, educational institutions, art, and culture.

Seminole Tribe of Florida (www.seminoletribe.com). This site contains a great deal of information on tribal lore, recipes, customs, history, present-day tourism and business enterprises, government, and services of the Florida Seminole. The tribal paper, the *Seminole Tribune*, can also be accessed at this site.

Will Rogers (www.willrogers.com). This site includes a biographical sketch of Rogers, some of his most famous quotes, his Hollywood performances, and links to the historical shrine in Colorado Springs, Colorado.

Works Consulted

Books

James Adair, *The History of the American Indians*. 1775. Reprint. New York: Johnson Reprint Corporation, 1968. This book provides a very detailed and comprehensive, although sometimes biased, account of the history and customs of the southeastern tribes during the mid-1700s.

Jesse Burt and Robert B. Ferguson, *Indians of the Southeast: Then and Now*. New York: Abingdon Press, 1973. This book examines the customs and culture of the southeastern tribes as a whole. The information is very specific and includes a great number of quotes from traders and explorers who lived among the tribes from the seventeenth to the nineteenth centuries.

Samuel Carter III, *Cherokee Sunset: A Nation Betrayed*. Garden City, NY: Doubleday, 1976. This book analyzes the reasons for the Cherokee removal, the events leading up to the tragedy, and the conflict that erupted within the Cherokee tribe over whether to move west or to stay and fight for their homeland.

H. B. Cushman, *The History of the Choctaw, Chickasaw, and Natchez Indians*. Greenville, TX: Headlight Printing House, 1899. This early comprehensive study of three southeastern tribes contains colorful descriptions of the social, political, and religious life of the Choctaw, Chickasaw, and Natchez peoples, both before and after European contact.

Editors of National Geographic Society, *The World of the American Indian*. Washington, DC: National Geographic Society, 1974. This book includes illustrations, photographs and information on individual tribes within regions. Language, housing, conflict with Europeans, and the removal are high-lighted.

Editors of Reader's Digest, *Through Indian Eyes*. Pleasantville, NY: Reader's Digest, 1995. This stunningly illustrated book is divided by regions and later by time periods, and covers in depth the history, culture, and spiritual beliefs of Native Americans. A very thorough examination of Native Americans in the twentieth century is provided, and the book has an astonishing number of quotes from Native Americans.

William Hartley and Ellen Hartley, *Osceola: The Unconquered Indian*. New York: Hawthorn Books, 1973. This book examines the life, deeds, and character of one of the most celebrated Seminole warriors of the nineteenth century, and includes interesting anec-dotes and stories.

Rodney L. Leftwich, *Arts and Crafts of the Cherokee*. Cullowhee, NC: Land-of-the-Sky Press, 1970. This book covers the process and variations of every art form created by the Cherokee, includ-ing weapons, woodwork, feathers, leather, metalwork, basketry, and pottery.

John R. Swanton, *Source Material for the Social and Ceremonial Life of the Choctaw Indians*. Bureau of American Ethnology, Bulletin 103. Washington, DC: Government Printing Office, 1931. This document offers some of the most thorough details about the Choctaw people by one of the premier ethnologists of the early twentieth century, who conducted many studies of Na-tive Americans for the U.S. government. It includes information on anything from how they built houses to food preparations to marriage and death customs.

Colin F. Taylor and William C. Sturtevant, consultants, *The Native Americans: The Indigenous People of North America*. New York: Smithmark, 1996. This book offers an overview of each region's tribes, including early history and how the cultures changed as a result of European influence.

Virgil J. Vogel, *American Indian Medicine*. Norman: University of Oklahoma Press, 1970. This book provides a fascinating glimpse of the healing methods used by Native Americans, including the role of medicine men in the community, the types of herbs used and what they were used for, native herbs that are used in similar ways today, and methods of treatment, such as steam baths and dream diagnosis.

Jon Manchip White, *Everyday Life of the North American Indian.* New York: Holmes and Meier, 1979. This book offers an overview of each aspect of Native American society, including chapters on the ancient mound builders, war customs, hunting, housing, farming, religion, and clan relationships.

Donald E. Worcester, ed., *Forked Tongues and Broken Treaties.* Caldwell, ID: Western Writers of America, 1975. This book closely examines the treaties made between the United States and Native Americans, covering the language of the treaties, reasons why they were worded the way they were, why Native Americans signed them, and the consequences of their signing.

Internet Sources

Judy Allen, director, *Bishinik*, Durant, OK. www.choctawnation. com/programs/Communications/bishinik.htm. This is a monthly publication sponsored by the Choctaw Nation of Oklahoma and is free to Choctaw tribal members. Both current and back issues include insightful and detailed articles on Choctaw culture and history.

The Cherokee Cultural Society of Houston, "John G. Burnett's Story of the Removal of the Cherokees," *Cherokee Messenger*, 1996. www.powersource.com/cherokee/burnett.html. This extremely vivid and moving account was given by Burnett on his eightieth birthday to his grandchildren, and highlights the tragedy of human suffering prior to and along the Trail of Tears, as well as the turn-of-the-century denial of responsibility by the U.S. government for the thousands of deaths that resulted.

Susan H. DePrim, "The Legal History of the Choctaw Nation, Before Removal," *Bishinik*, February 1996. www.isd.net/mboucher/

choctaw/claw2.htm. This fascinating article looks at the role of myths and legends in keeping the social order within tribal communities by teaching values and the consequences of individual behavior.

Gale Group, "Women's History," 1999. www.galegroup.com/ library/res. This site includes a brief biography of Wilma Mankiller, the first female principal chief of the Oklahoma Cherokee, and includes vivid personal details of how she overcame great tragedy and dedicated herself to serving her people.

Len Green, "Choctaw Funeral Customs Were Changing Through the Years," *Bishinik*, July 1979. www.isd.net/mboucher/choctaw/ burial1.htm. This article contains details on the Bonepickers and other customs that were not only characteristic of the Choctaw, but most of the southeastern tribes.

Indigenous Peoples' Literature, "Tsalagi (Cherokee) Literature," 1999. www.indians.org/welker/cherokee.htm. This article includes anecdotes and primary quotes from many Native Americans covering the topics of spirituality, heritage, the future, and the past.

Charlie Jones, "Memorial Exercises at the Grave of Pushmataha," *Bishinik*, November 1987. www.isd.net/mboucher/choctaw/ push1.htm. This picturesque article describes the warrior and chief of the Choctaw, Pushmataha—including his pride, admiration of the white man, oratory rebuttal to Tecumseh's union of Indian tribes, and participation in the War of 1812.

Ken Martin, "History of the Cherokee—1700 Through the Revolutionary War," 1996. http://pages.tca.net/martikw/1700thro.html. These pages cover details of the political and economic relationship between whites and Native Americans during the eighteenth century.

W. B. Morrison, "Story of Pushmataha, Historic Choctaw Chief," *Bishinik*, www.isd.net/mboucher/choctaw/push2.htm. This article further examines the character of this esteemed Choctaw chief, including his encouragement of educating Choctaw youths in the European way.

Edna L. Paisano, "The American Indian, Eskimo, and Aleut Population," U.S. Census Bureau, January 29, 1999. www.census.gov/population/www/pop-profile/amerind.html. This census report provides statistical information on the American Indian, Eskimo, and Aleut population.

Michael Rutledge, "Forgiveness in the Age of Forgetfulness," 1995. http://pages.tca.net/martikw/law.html. This document offers an insightful analysis of the workings of law and justice within tribal communities of the Southeast, both before and after European contact. Interesting stories highlight the emphasis on clan loyalty and the revenge system.

Index

Picture Credits

Cover photo: George Mobley/NGS Image Collection
Archive Photos, 12, 27, 49, 50
Baldwin Photo/FPG International, 28
©Billy E. Barnes/FPG International, 9
©Tom Bean/Corbis, 91
©Patrick Bennett/Corbis, 89
©Bettman/Corbis, 85
©Corbis, 33, 36
©Lee Foster/FPG International, 13
FPG International, 7, 37
©Willie Hill/FPG International, 80
Library of Congress, 30, 53, 56, 61, 62, 64, 78
©Buddy Mays/Corbis, 46
Museum of the Cherokee, 31
©The Newberry Library/Stock Montage, 68, 69
North Wind, 43, 58
©Stan Osolinski/FPG International, 18
©Prints Old and Rare, 41
©Stock Montage, 21
©Nik Wheeler/Corbis, 23
Woolaroc Museum, 73

About the Author

Christina M. Girod received her undergraduate degree from the University of California at Santa Barbara. She worked with speech- and language-impaired students and taught elementary school for six years in Denver, Colorado. She has written scores of short biographies as well as organizational and country profiles for educational multimedia materials. The topics she has covered include both historical and current sketches of politicians, humanitarians, environmentalists, and entertainers. *Native Americans of the Southeast* is her first book. Girod lives in San Diego, California, with her husband, Jon Pierre, and daughter, Joni.